CW01617482

The nsci Stop-Smoking Handbook

International Edition

Use the Handbook in conjunction with the videos on the Institute's website at www.thensci.info

"Since 1990 the NSCI, through its research into nicotine addiction and its network of clinics, has been making a growing contribution to the health of the nation."

Rt Hon Lord Ennals
Secretary of State for Health, 1976-9

First published in Great Britain in 2011 by the NSCI.

ISBN 978 0 9526343 5 5

National Smoking Cessation Institute
P O Box 365, Hove, BN3 3SE, UK
handbook@stopsmoking.coop
www.thensci.info

Printed and bound by CPI Group (UK) Ltd, Croydon, CR0 4YY

Dedicated
to the tens of thousands of smokers
who have taught me everything I know

CONTENTS

Part One

First learn a lot of things without which you are doomed to failure

Part Two

Now follow the plan

Extra bits

Before you Start

Here are two promises:

- I am not going to lecture you about the evils of smoking, because I would be very surprised if you don't know all of that already.
- No matter what you have already read about stopping smoking, I am going to tell you things you don't know.

OK, so what do I know about helping people to stop smoking? Am I a reformed smoker who wants to save people from their fate? No. Well, I'm an ex-smoker as it happens but your fate is your business and I don't think my personal story is of the slightest interest to you so we'll just skip it.

More importantly, I'm the Research Director of the National Smoking Cessation Institute, and what we, as a research co-operative, don't know about this subject isn't worth knowing.

Now, this is how the Handbook works. First, you read Part One, and then you read Part Two. It's not difficult.

Part One covers everything you need to know before you attempt to stop smoking. Why do you need to know these things? Well, they say knowledge is power and it's a cliché but it's a good one, because the biggest single factor in failing to achieve something is lack of knowledge. An example: how likely would you be to pass a driving test without someone teaching you how to drive? I accept that the idea of learning how to stop smoking might be a novel one to you but get used to it.

An example: how can eating tomatoes make it harder, for some people, to stop smoking? No, this is not a joke, it's science. If you don't know the answer, and I suspect you don't, you are going to enjoy Part One.

So, to Part Two. No-one can create a plan that is going to work for everyone and put it into a book, so I need you to bear with me on this one. Part Two has things for you to do that will, I promise, bring you closer to stopping. Can I promise that you will read the last page and stop? No, of course not. Whether you stop smoking or not is not up to me, it's up to you, and I mention this for a good reason. You smoke for a number of reasons, which of course I shall be going into in some depth, but no-one makes you smoke. Whether you stop is actually in your power. So don't abdicate responsibility to me. You could stop smoking right now. In this Handbook I'm going to make the impossible possible, and if it already was then I'm going to make what was hard easier.

You have the Handbook for one of three reasons:

- You are going to read it and try to stop smoking with its help. OK, but feel free to e-mail us for advice.

- You are going to try stopping with a drug product from your GP or pharmacist, or with a non-NSCI therapist. You will find some advice about integrating the plan with these products and therapies in Part Two.

- You have been given the Handbook as part of one of the Institute's programmes, in which case just follow the instructions you have been given with that programme.

Read this Now. And I do Mean Now

Now, before you go any further, I want you to turn straight to Project 2 in Part Two. This is because that project is done twice. First you answer the questions as you feel before you read Part One, and then you answer them again after Part One. Sorry if that sounds complicated but it's not really and it's well worth doing. Don't do any of the rest of Part Two yet, will you? That wouldn't work at all.

PART ONE

The Tutorials

Tutorial One

Why people smoke when it makes no sense

The tobacco industry has an overwhelming imperative if it's going to maintain its market. It must make smoking appear normal. If it seems normal to people, there is always going to be a conflict between smoking and stopping. As long as smokers can be convinced that smoking really is normal, they are going to disbelieve the messages they get about the importance of stopping. As long as children get messages that it's normal, they are going to ignore the warnings they get against starting.

How do the pushers achieve this? Well, to a large extent it's historical. Smoking wasn't an issue for centuries. It was only with the introduction of the machinery of mass production that the nature of smoking changed. Before that, poor people, which was most of the population, smoked pipes and rich people smoked cigars, and by people by and large I mean men.

When it became possible to produce ready-made cigarettes in factories, this opened up the market enormously, because now it was possible to sell smoking to poor people at a price they could afford. Before that, poor people died of poverty, but now they were starting to become less poor as a result of a range of social and economic factors, so they could live longer and die of other things instead. Now, they wanted what rich people had, and rich people had cigars. Cigarette means what? It means a small cigar. It's what you smoke when you can't buy the real thing, but the very name made it an aspirational thing.

So smoking was a big thing long before we really understood exactly how dangerous it was. Now, when some food is found to have health risks the government bans it instantly. A one in a million chance of catching something? Clear the shelves instantly. No cost is too high to protect the public, even from a small danger like that. BSE? Kill all the cattle. Tobacco causes lung cancer? Sell it in sweetshops.

Yes, it's a funny old world. Tobacco is so dangerous it must, by law, come with a warning that it's going to kill you, but the same government that insists on that lets tobacco companies push it to children.

What does that mean? Think about it. Go into a sweetshop. What do you see in the bottom row of the sweet display? The cheap sweets (a farthing in my day, so now you know how old I am). Then, as you look up, which a child does because they're starting from a low point, you see the more expensive sweets that you aspire to as you grow up and they keep getting more expensive until the display stops and the eye keeps going up until it sees ... what? That's right, cigarettes. The tobacco companies give those displays free of charge to the retailers, because they know that's where they will be placed. The tobacco companies are targeting children, grooming them to become smokers by telling them that buying tobacco is as normal as buying sweets.

It is true that, as I write this, the UK government is making noises about stopping this, after we have been banging on about it for years but of course it's got absolutely nothing to do with that, oh no, but even so. The fact remains that generations of children have been taught that smoking is normal, that it's what you grow into when you outgrow sweets, in fact that it's something to look forward to.

You went through it, I went through it, we were being manipulated right from the beginning and we never knew it and our parents never knew it.

Fast forward to now, and take a walk along any urban street. Look down at the pavement and what do you see? Yes, your feet, but apart from those? Cigarette stubs. The pavement is the world's largest ashtray. That's an issue for local councils, who try but fail to do anything about it. The effect, though, is that you just can't get away from seeing the evidence of smoking.

In fact, it's getting worse. Regulations about not smoking in buildings mean that more and more people are hanging round outside, on the pavement, smoking, being seen by children who wouldn't have seen them before when they were safely inside the pub or the office, places where children don't go. It's a kind of bonus for the tobacco companies.

The children just don't stand a chance. And neither, come to that, do you, because you see all these things too. Go into a sweetshop to buy a newspaper and you will see the cigarettes displayed, and what that says to you is that it's normal because if it weren't it wouldn't be allowed, and this militates against everything your brain has been saying about stopping. You know you're not supposed to smoke, but the messages you get all day, in the newsagent's, in the street, wherever, is that smoking is normal.

People smoke because other people smoke.

Now back to the title of this tutorial. There are actually three questions:

- Why do people try smoking in the first place?
- Why do they persist with smoking?
- Why do they keep smoking for years?

Why did you try smoking?

Here's another question first: if a child asked you for a cigarette because they wanted to try smoking, would you give them one? I've asked a lot of smokers this question in my work and the answer has only ever been no. You know that trying a cigarette leads to becoming a smoker, and your experience of being one of those is that you wouldn't want a child to do it.

If only someone had explained that to you when you tried it. Well, of course even back then the chances are you knew it wasn't a good idea, but on the other hand it rather depends on what you call a good idea. Becoming a lifelong smoker and spending two thousand pounds a year and getting emphysema and surviving on an oxygen machine while you wait to die isn't a good idea, but somehow that wasn't how you thought about it when you were fourteen.

What you saw was people all around you smoking and not dying. What you didn't know is that smokers, at the end of their lives, aren't walking around smoking, they're at home or in hospital coughing their guts up where you can't see them. Not all of them, of course, but a lot of them.

Why did you try that first cigarette? Well, almost certainly because someone you knew smoked and either they encouraged you to or perhaps they didn't need to because you wanted to do what they were doing anyway. So the short answer to why people try the first cigarette is because they see other people smoking. This means, by the way, that every child who sees you smoking is being taught to smoke one day, so actually you don't need to give a child a cigarette. Just smoking in public means you're doing the unpaid advertising the tobacco companies know you will do, grooming the next generation for their product.

Why did you persist with smoking?

There's lots more about this further on in the Handbook but for now the simple answer is that you learned how to smoke, which in medical terms means you switched off your body's ability to tell that cigarette smoke is poisonous, which is what we call adaptation and you call addiction (but lots more about all that, in detail, I promise you, because you really need to know this stuff), and having done that you simply carried on doing it so you became habituated to smoking and then you became what we call psychologically dependent, which in a nutshell means you learned to believe in smoking as a good thing, which is probably where you are up to now.

Most youngsters try smoking but a lot of them don't persist with it. They don't like the first cigarette and they just decide not to bother. It does, after all, make a lot of sense. Why would you persist with something you don't like? Actually, it's not a rhetorical question. Why do some young people persist with something they don't like? It can, surely, only be because of some need to conform to what other people are doing. And people who need to conform are, by definition, less sure of themselves than people who don't. In other words, smoking, like all drug taking, targets the weak.

That's not a criticism of you. I fell for it too. But it does point to a fact that you must consider when you come to stopping smoking. Drugs are about control. The pusher needs to control you, because it's how they make their profit. You fell for it when you tried the first cigarette, and you fell for it again when you persisted in smoking even when the experience wasn't a good one. The tobacco companies are depending on you being weak now. Are you going to give in to that abuse again?

Why do you keep smoking?

Once you are addicted, and the addiction has created the psychological dependence, you are stuck. You believe in smoking and that belief is reinforced with every cigarette because every cigarette satisfies the physical need for nicotine, the addiction. Now, there is every reason to carry on smoking and almost none for stopping. Except that despite all of this there is a nagging doubt. Another part of your brain, a part that tobacco doesn't have the ability to control, isn't completely convinced. And, of course, everyone says you shouldn't do it. You know that but you fight the logic and win. You see it on the pack every time you light up, that it's going to make you impotent, but hey, who cares? Impotence is cool.

No, seriously, why don't people take any notice of the death threat on cigarette packs? Because they know it's true, on the intellectual level, but on the emotional level there are stronger messages whizzing round in their heads that tell them to ignore it.

There are two ways of knowing something (probably more than two for all I know) - you can have intellectual knowledge and then there is emotional knowledge. The logic that smoking is a bad thing is irrefutable and every smoker knows that, but every smoker's brain is under the control of a drug that changes their perception of that knowledge, that makes it hard to FEEL that smoking is bad.

At the Institute we do a lot of talking to smokers. I personally have spent many happy hours just talking to smokers even in the street, learning from them. What is so depressing is the overwhelming number who say they don't want to stop, but accept they are on an addictive drug that is likely to be very bad for them. It's like they are saying look, I'm talking nonsense and you and I both know that but let me just go on believing it.

This is the true impact of drug addiction, the human brain's ability to know it is trapped but its inability to figure out that it matters.

Smoking is irrational, but so is buying national lottery tickets. You know you're not going to win but you still do it. Believing the unbelievable is an interesting human characteristic. We've got the biggest brains on the planet but we're the only life form that goes bungee jumping.

Inevitably, the question, why do people keep smoking, is tied in with the fact that if you don't keep smoking you have to stop, and is of course the subject of the next tutorials. When you think about it, you do what you want and you don't do what you don't want, and if you're doing something that you stop wanting to do you stop doing it. It's kind of simple. But stopping smoking becomes more than not doing something, it becomes doing something. The stopping becomes an active process.

People don't like change. You might want to move house but where you live now has the advantage of being comfortable, if only because you know it so well. People don't like relationships to split up in part because it means upheaval and while it's not my subject I'm quite sure some people stay in a bad relationship for that reason.

There's no such thing as an adult smoker who thinks that what they are doing makes sense, or is right, so what we've got in the UK alone is 14 million people who are doing something they know is wrong. I don't mean wrong like breaking the speed limit which is illegal and morally wrong, but wrong solely in that it is self-harm. Now it is possible that these 14 million people have something wrong with their brains that makes them do this but I doubt it. And yet, in a way, they do have something wrong with their brains. Your brain is under the influence of an addictive drug, and it's also under the influence of a society that says that's OK (it must be, because that society condones its sale and consumption).

So if 14 million smokers all have something in common that makes them keep doing something they can't defend, and it's not insanity, what is it? Well, here's a clue. It's got something to do with cigarettes.

Fascinating Fact Number 1

It is harder for women to stop smoking than for men. This is because addiction is a function of the immune system and women's regular hormonal changes can make the addiction deeper. This in turn can create greater psychological dependence.

Use this space to make any comments or note any reminders for yourself.

Tutorial Two

Why smokers don't want to stop

If I took a clipboard out onto the street and asked smokers if they want to stop, I can tell you what the answer would be. Ninety percent of them, minimum, would say no.

If I then asked them another question, which is have you ever tried to stop smoking, almost all of them would say yes.

(By the way, how do I know this? Because I've done it.)

So we seem to have a wee conflict here. If they don't want to stop why have they tried? It doesn't make sense. Except that it does. When they say they don't want to stop, they don't actually mean they don't want to stop. It's a classic case of saying the wrong thing, another interesting human characteristic. What they actually mean is that they don't believe they CAN stop, because they keep failing, so they interpret that as leave me alone will you. But excuse me, it's just not good enough.

Saying you don't want to stop should mean that, not I

can't so I don't want to. You can't win the lottery but you want to. So far then, I've just proved the opposite of what I called this tutorial. I seem to be saying people say they want to stop when they don't. Confused? Just wait.

The problem isn't with the question, it's with the words. You might already have noticed (but thinking about it, no, probably you haven't) that I never talk about giving up smoking. I always talk about stopping. Why is that? It's quite simple, really. We associate giving up with loss, and my colleagues and I do not believe someone who stops smoking is losing anything. Quite the opposite, they are gaining something, so we don't call it giving up. But you do. Everyone does.

Do you want to give things up? No, because it implies loss, as I said. OK, then, let's use my word, stopping. Do you want to stop smoking? Aha, slightly more tricky, but I can do tricky. Just watch.

What you want if my guess is right, based on the indisputable fact that you're reading this, is to be someone who doesn't smoke. If you could wave a magic wand and you had never started smoking I think you would go for it, with some reservations perhaps but not many. What I'm saying here is that just about every smoker wants to be a non-smoker. What they don't want is to become a non-smoker.

Pardon? Read that sentence again, and this time put the emphasis on become. There's nothing wrong with being a non-smoker, but there's everything wrong, apparently (because you haven't managed to do it yet) with becoming one. Therefore, the problem isn't in the being, it's in the becoming. The act of STOPPING is what you don't want.

You don't want to stop smoking. You do want to be someone who doesn't smoke. I know, I'm fussy about words, but that's something you're going to have to get used to, because if we don't call a spade a spade we end up trying to dig the garden with a hoe. Or something.

Giving up, stopping, I could argue it comes to the same thing, going through something you don't want to go through, losing something you believe in, even though you know you shouldn't believe in it, so now you're full of conflict but then drug taking, which, to call that spade by its true name is what we're talking about here, is full of conflict. The tobacco companies legally sell a product that just doesn't make any sense, the only product with a death threat printed on the pack that doesn't stop people buying it. So if anyone knows it's full of holes, it's the pushers. They know very well what they're doing to you and you suspect what they're doing to you but you're not completely convinced, which is how they get away with it.

If you look at it like that there would be some argument that you would have to be crazy to smoke. Actually, it's a completely reasonable statement, you WOULD have to be crazy to smoke, but on the other hand if we take that statement seriously rather than as a joke we've got a problem, because it would mean that twenty-one percent of adults in the US are certifiably insane, and that, let's face it, is unlikely. What we've got is a lot of people who are perfectly rational most of the time but do something that isn't rational at all, which they can't explain so they don't try. Now that's what I call crazy.

You know you can't justify smoking, but at the same time you can't stop. That, in a nutshell, is what psychological dependence means. The addiction to nicotine creates the belief not only that you can't stop smoking but that you don't want to, but it can only do this on one level, which is really interesting. On the intellectual level you know you want to stop but on the emotional level you know you don't. It's a cunning trick. Addiction can only control you on the emotional level. It can't change logic, it can't change white to black, it can't make smoking make sense. It can only make you afraid, and that is exactly what it is supposed to do, because by being afraid you are in the control of tobacco and the pushers who sell it.

Sometimes you say you do want to stop, which is true because you know for sure, in your saner moments, that it's right, and sometimes you say you don't want to stop, but those are the moments when tobacco is controlling your thoughts. You have a brain that has been developed and finely honed over hundreds of thousands of years, and it has the power to overcome the fear the tobacco companies impose on you.

When you say you don't want to stop smoking, or even that you're not sure you want to stop, you don't actually believe that. I know this because countless times I have challenged people, face to face, over their beliefs, and they have always crumbled. I can make grown men weep with this one, and in the end they give in to me. Not, actually, because I have any special power, I admit (sadly) but because the logic simply cannot be argued with.

The ninety percent of smokers on the street who say they don't want to stop smoking are lying. No, alright, they're not actually lying, because that would be deliberate, but they are obfuscating, which sounds nicer.

Every smoker is afraid to stop, and that fear is something you are going to be reading a lot more about later because it's the biggest single reason why people make themselves believe they don't want to stop. Even when they admit they do want to stop, and they try to and fail, it is almost always the fear of stopping that has caused that failure.

The fact is, there is almost no smoker who is glad they do it. Everyone who smokes wants to stop.

Including you.

Case Study

A lady came in to our Hove StopShop one day. Well, she just put her head round the door and said I don't want to come in dear because I don't want to stop smoking, I just want to say what a marvellous idea this shop is and keep up the good work.

Well, in the end she came in and we chatted, and I said there was no way I would try to convince her to stop smoking, it's not our job to do that, it's our job to help people who ask us to. She was in her eighties, she said, (the most glamorous octogenarian I've ever seen, or am I getting old myself?) and had never stopped smoking, or wanted to.

I talked about our work, and inevitably we got on to the subject of why people think they don't want to stop not because they don't want to stop but because they misunderstand what they feel about smoking because they are addicted, and she said yes, she could see the point, and there the conversation ended. It was just one of those nice chats that I personally enjoy so much and learn a little bit more from.

Two weeks later she popped her head round the door again and I happened to be in the shop again, and she said remember me, which I did, and she came in and we chatted again. I've stopped smoking, she said, and then she laughed when she saw my reaction. Why, I asked. Because, she said, I have never been an adult non-smoker. I just wanted to test your idea, the one where you said maybe I'm smoking not because I want to but because I'm addicted, and I got to thinking that before I die I want to know if that's true, if I'm actually living a lie.

And? And, she said, I now know that's what I was doing. So will you go back to smoking, now that you proved the point, I asked. No, she said, what would be the point?

Alright, it's not a real case in as much as she wasn't a patient of ours, but somehow this old lady gave us something more than financial reward, she gave us renewed belief in what we are doing.

You might, by the way, want to know the reasons people give, when I talk to them with that clipboard in my hand, for not wanting to stop smoking, because you have probably said one or more of them yourself at some time.

Because I enjoy it

There's a tutorial later in the Handbook that explains why you think you enjoy smoking when it's not true, but for now think about this.

Calculate the financial cost, each year, of smoking. Let's call smoking a hobby you enjoy but it's time to work out not if you can afford it but if, which is different, you can justify it on the grounds purely of enjoyment. No, I know you already know you can't afford it, but don't spoil my fun.

Say you smoke 20 a day, and that costs you, let's say, £6. That's £2190 a year. Now, suppose you were making a decision at this point whether you could take on a commitment of £2190 a year, not for a child's education, or for a new car or anything else, but for something that brings the pleasure of smoking, whatever you believe that pleasure to be. I want you to ask yourself if you believe you can justify that pleasure at a cost of £2190 a year. Forget whether it's a real pleasure or not, and just assume it is. What would you rather have, right now, smoking or a new car? Smoking or a great family holiday every year? Smoking or, to go to extremes, supporting the education of several children in Africa?

If you believe you don't want to stop smoking because you like it too much, you need to challenge that belief in a very real way, because right now that pleasure is costing you a family holiday, and I want you to ask yourself which pleasure you would rather have.

The problem with this whole idea, though, is that you don't enjoy smoking (which I'm going to prove later), you just tell yourself you do. It's an excuse. But it's an excuse that has gone past its sell-by date, isn't it?

Because I've tried and I can't stop

Of course you can stop. I've already touched on this but

come on, how can any sane person say they can't STOP doing something? What you mean is you haven't succeeded yet, but that's not the same thing at all. What you have failed to do in the past has absolutely nothing to do with what you might achieve in the future. What that failure does, though, is convince you to stop trying, and it combines with all the other wrong beliefs to do this. Children say they can't so they don't want to but you are not a child. You are an intelligent adult and it is time to take responsibility. If you concede defeat now, you are giving the tobacco companies the right to destroy your life, and I won't let you do that.

Because I need to smoke when I'm stressed

Of course you do, everyone does. Everyone knows that smoking makes you less stressed.

Except that it's all rubbish. It's not a reason, it's another excuse. There's a whole tutorial on this later because stress is the biggest excuse smokers have for starting again when they have stopped, and if you don't take this on board now you are doomed, doomed I say, so listen up. Smoking does not reduce stress, it increases it. If you believe you can't stop smoking because you are stressed you are in deep deep trouble, because you're facing the wrong way in a one-way street. By the time you have finished the Handbook I never want to hear you saying again that you can't stop smoking because you're stressed. Got it?

Because I'm too young for it to matter

The median age for smokers in our clinics is mid-40s. It

takes, apparently, this long for the average smoker to twig to what is happening to them. If young people understood, they wouldn't start smoking in the first place. It's as if once they start they are committed to losing, say, twenty years to tobacco.

The sad result is that when they get to 40 or so they find it such a struggle to stop. I very rarely meet a smoker in their 40s who doesn't regret starting. The logic, though, is that if smoking is bad for you, at the age of 20, or even 30, you are strong enough to get away with it. It is, of course, quite idiotic, because what the thirty-year-old smoker doesn't see is first the damage they have done because it is after all inside them, and second the difficulties they are storing up with stopping when they are older. Saying you're too young to stop smoking is an oxymoron.

Because I'm too old for it to matter

An 85-year-old man once said to me he was too old to stop smoking. What, he said, would be the point? Most people in the medical profession seem to buy that idea. Well I don't. I said to this man, OK, you're going to die, we all are, but to some extent you've got a choice about how you do it. You can increase the chance of dying with an oxygen mask on your face, struggling to breathe, or you increase the chance of dying peacefully when your heart stops as you sleep. Which, I asked, would you prefer?

To tell anyone they are too old to worry about stopping smoking is simply patronising. I'm not saying they should stop, because I have never in my work told anyone they should stop, but I am saying, if this is you, that it is unintelligent to opt for death by tobacco.

So it looks like I've come full circle. People say they don't want to stop smoking, but they're wrong. Whatever the excuse they make, the fact remains, and at this point you might want to test yourself with this question – if you wish you had never started smoking, at the very least if you would decline to encourage a child to start smoking, then you wish you could turn the clock back and be someone who doesn't smoke.

Well, you can't change the past, but you can change the future.

You have to want to stop

In my list of silly myths, this comes pretty well at the top. I mean, excuse me, it doesn't even mean anything.

If you wanted to stop smoking, you wouldn't be reading this Handbook. Aha, you're thinking, he's wrong, I'm reading it BECAUSE I want to stop smoking. No you're not, you're reading it because you want me to convince you you can, which isn't the same thing at all.

If I haven't made this clear so far, I'll have one more go. No-one wants to stop smoking. Given that we're talking about stopping something, not starting something, if you wanted to stop doing anything you would do it.

Aha from me this time, because what we now have to talk about is what wanting means. If I want a fried egg sandwich with HP sauce (and now I've told you one of my secrets) I'll have one. If, on the other hand, we're all out of eggs and it's snowing out here and ER is on, then suddenly I don't want a fried egg sandwich. Not enough, anyway. And that's the point, isn't it?

Now I'm going to contradict myself (get used to it). Everyone wants to stop smoking. A bit. But not enough, in most cases, to overcome the fear of doing it and the trouble of doing it, because it's always easier not to bother, and convince yourself, as I do as I settle in front of the TV, that you didn't want a fried egg sandwich, or to stop smoking.

So look, don't worry if you don't think you want to stop. I've already proved you do, but now what we have is that you don't want it enough. Well, it's a start. All you've got to do now is make it easier so that you want it more. And that's where I might be able to help you.

I'm not ready

No, I don't suppose you are, because let's face it if you were you would stop and you wouldn't be reading this, so the fact that you are reading it means pretty well by definition that you're not ready.

But what does not ready actually mean? I'm not ready to go to the dentist, but I go. Why? Well, because I have to. Why aren't I ready? Because I'm afraid (I admit it, I'm a coward). I'm not ready, when you stop to think about it, is just plain silly. It really means I'm afraid to do it. It can't mean anything else. I'm not ready to save £2000 a year and improve my health. Oh really? Well, that's easy to understand. I would also have to steel myself to do that.

No-one is ready to do something that's hard. You're not

ready to stop smoking for the simple reason that you are afraid to face it. You can try arguing with me but you will be wrong, so save your breath. Admit you are afraid, admit it is making you say silly things, and pull yourself together.

Because I've got to die somehow

Come on, am I supposed to take that seriously? It's the ultimate addict's nonsense. If it doesn't matter how you die, or even when, why do you look before you cross the road? Getting killed by a 38-tonne truck is, I promise you, a far easier and quicker way to die than waiting for your lungs to stop working.

So why does anyone even say it? Because they don't want to face stopping, because they are afraid. Saying you've got to die somehow so why not enjoy it doesn't make sense at all, because you don't enjoy it, which you are going to have conclusively proven in the Handbook.

I've even had smokers say they might as well die doing something they enjoy, and then admit, practically in the same breath, that they don't enjoy smoking. I ask you, is that the way an intelligent adult thinks?

Because I like chewing gum

Pardon? Well, imagine you have the habit of chewing gum very regularly. You might say: I enjoy gum, I like to hand it round in company, I chew it when I'm bored, or as a reward, I like gum after a meal, and chewing helps me to relax. Alright, so far all of this is perhaps true. Now, imagine that one morning you wake up and the headline in every newspaper is that something people are in the habit of using every day has been discovered to be the major cause of death from cancer and heart disease, and that thing is chewing gum, that gum is killing three hundred people a day.

Is it conceivable that for anyone the benefits of chewing would outweigh the danger? Would gum chewers say I really want to stop but I can't, because I need it to relax? Chewing gum would instantly be banned by the government because there would be no profit in it for them. Either that or they would tax it, and if that meant that chewing gum was going to cost, say, £2000 a year people would stop buying it anyway because no-one needs to chew gum that much. And that's the point. No-one needs to chew gum. You can have all the same habits with gum as with tobacco, all the same associations with pleasure and relaxation, but what you will never have for it is a need. You would, in short, stop chewing gum because you're not addicted to it.

Fascinating Fact Number 2

There is a myth that tobacco companies add something to their cigarettes to make them more addictive. They don't, because they don't need to. There is enough nicotine in the lightest cigarette to keep you addicted without adding anything. There must be - otherwise people who smoke light cigarettes would find it easier to stop than people who smoke high-tar cigarettes, but they don't.

Use this space to make any comments or
note any reminders for yourself.

Tutorial Three

Why it's hard to stop, and stay stopped

Stopping smoking is hard because most people do it wrong. They see a new product in the news and go straight to their GP to ask for it. They see a therapist advertising stop in one hour, guaranteed, and they rush off to give him their money. They have no idea what their problem is, why they can't stop smoking, and they act surprised when the wonder cure doesn't work.

So that's why so many people fail to stop with any given method, but there's a more fundamental question. Why can't you just stop? Why do you need help? We ask people this question when they ring us about one of our programmes. Here's a typical conversation:

'So, how many cigarettes do you smoke?'

'Oh, about twenty.'

'I see. What have you tried so far?'

'Well, you know, patches, gum, that sort of thing.'

'And did they help?'

'Not really.'

'I see, so what do you think the problem is?'

'What do you mean?'

'I mean why can't you stop smoking?'

'I've no idea. I wish I did but I just can't figure it out.'

'Really?'

'Uhuh.'

'OK, let's try a different approach. Do you think you are addicted to nicotine?'

'Oh, of course I am.'

Now I'm pretty sure if I asked a heroin user why he couldn't come off heroin his immediate response would be that he's addicted to heroin, and he would probably say it in a sarcastic kind of way as if it's a daft question, which it is. He's addicted, so he can't stop taking it. Cause and effect, simple.

Ask a smoker, though, and for some reason that eludes me he is unable to make the connection between being addicted to nicotine and his inability to stop smoking. I've been doing this job for more years than is healthy and still I don't get it, why smokers don't make the connection.

So am I saying that's it, that addiction is the reason why you can't stop smoking, pure and simple?

No, I'm not. Addiction, as you will be learning, is far far more important than anyone has ever told you before, whether it's another stop-smoking book or a professional who should know this stuff. But it is not, on its own, the whole problem. Addiction can be overcome, even without treatment (which now exists) if you just don't smoke for long enough. I could tell you now that after four days of not smoking, not passive smoking, and not eating tomatoes (tomatoes again, how interesting) you will not be addicted to nicotine, and that will be the end of the problem, except it won't. What I will be going into in some detail is the psychological dependence that is created by the addiction and why this dependence stops you trying to stop smoking, or scuppers an attempt, or makes you go back to smoking after you have succeeded in stopping.

Now I have to say something you are not going to like. Once a smoker, always someone who used to be a smoker. If you think that means once a smoker always a smoker it doesn't. It means what it says. Being addicted, to anything, turns your brain to mush. Stopping smoking doesn't unmush your brain. It can't. The human brain is not capable of being hooked on a drug and then coming off it as if it was never on it in the first place. Your brain will remember smoking until the day you die. The tobacco companies know this. They know that a hell of a lot of people who came off their drug are going to go back on it. Without that they simply couldn't make a profit.

Psychological dependence means not only that you believe in smoking but that you don't believe in stopping.

OK, you believe you should perhaps, and you might even believe it's possible, even if only for other people, but allowing yourself to become addicted to nicotine has done permanent and irreparable damage to your brain. It has, effectively, taken over control of you. You might well recognise the feeling. A lot of the smokers who come to us say that is the worst thing about it, being controlled by tobacco. Actually, they're not as controlled as they think, but that's another facet of the control. It makes you believe it controls you when it doesn't, it can't, because you're an intelligent adult who has control over your life.

Alright, not complete control over everything, but certainly control over what you put in your mouth. The really really clever thing about tobacco is that it creates the belief that it controls you. It makes you lose the belief that you will ever be able to do anything about it.

I know this because so many smokers tell us about their previous failed attempts in language that is quite instructive. They say I did so and so but it didn't work. Didn't work? What on Earth does that mean? They're under the control of nicotine so they buy some product or service which promises to give them back control, but in fact they can take back control when they want. If you buy something that is supposed to give you control, but you do absolutely nothing about exercising your right to make your own decisions, well excuse me but you deserve to fail and you also deserve to waste the money you just spent.

Look, let me put this another way (please, I hear you say). Imagine a woman has an abusive husband. She makes excuses for him. He only hits me, she says, when he's drunk, and that's only once a day. He loves me really. He says so.

He says so? Oh, well that's alright then, it must be true. The poor woman is being abused and the worst abuse is that her husband has prevented her from seeing that she's being abused. That is true control, and it's how drugs work. They beat you up but then they tell you they love you and you believe them because, remember, your brain has turned to mush.

If I had a pound for every smoker I've had the following conversation with, I wouldn't need to do this, you know, writing to make a living.

'OK, why can't you stop smoking?'

'Um, well with me it's just a habit.'

'Really?'

'Yeh, I wish I could break it.'

'OK, I'll tell you how to break it, for free, and I'm not joking.'

(So I tell them how to break the habit, which I'm not going to tell you now because if I do you might not read the rest of the Handbook.)

'Oh, well, yes, you're right.'

'I know. So, now tell me, what's the real reason you can't stop?'

'Well you know I'm a librarian. It's a very stressful job.'

'Uhuh, and are you saying that this stress is the reason why you can't stop smoking?'

'Er, yes?'

(So then I tell them some home truths about stress, which, you've got it, I'm not going to tell you now.)

'OK, we've dealt with that, what else is there?'

'Well because of the stress, I go out drinking and that's why I smoke.'

(Now I tell them what to do about that, simple stuff, they could have thought of it themselves except they're so stressed.)

'So, now, are there any other reasons?'

And so the conversation goes on. We cover addiction, and I explain this is the root of the problem, which they're not always convinced about because they've read that addiction doesn't matter, well excuse me, try telling a heroin user that.

But I said before that addiction isn't the only reason you can't stop smoking, and it isn't, because addiction, as I've already said, creates the psychological dependence that makes you believe you can't stop, and this is the point.

I have a confession to make. Back in 1991, when we started using the treatment for nicotine addiction that we have, we just gave it to people and expected them to stop smoking. Well, they were no longer addicted so what else could there be? There was in fact, believe it or not, no literature on the complex relationship between addiction and dependence. Reams and reams of research papers, shelfloads of books, but no answer to the real problems, and we had to learn the hard way, by which I mean some of the people phoned and said they weren't succeeding.

It was a bitter blow, but we knew the treatment was important so we learned about dependence from our patients and then it all worked the way it was supposed to.

It is, in short, this relationship between addiction and dependence that makes it hard to stop smoking. I'm going to be explaining both subjects in a lot of detail in later tutorials, so by the time you finish Part One and you're ready to start the projects in Part Two you will have a completely different understanding about why you can't stop, and how to tackle those reasons logically and successfully. I think I've said it before but I'm afraid I have to say it again, knowledge is power. With this knowledge you will have the power to stop smoking.

Allocating the time to stop smoking

You wouldn't think that stopping doing something would be a project you would need to allocate time for, but with smoking it is.

Not doing this is a reason why some people fail. It's a bit difficult for someone who no longer smokes, like me, to get your head round this one, but there are smokers who 'forget' not to smoke. You might wonder how they could do that. I mean, surely, if you don't have cigarettes and you have decided not to smoke there can't be a lot to forget. Some people say oh well I forgot I was supposed to be stopping and a friend offered me one and I just took it.

Yes, well, when you put it like that it's understandable. Except for two things. First, had you told your friend right at the beginning that you were stopping they might not have offered you one. And if you had decided that if you ever smoke you will address how you respond to it (which is explained in Part Two), then you wouldn't have made the mistake of smoking a second one.

In other words, if you had really thought it through, allocated time and space in your brain to this matter, you wouldn't have made the mistake of smoking, or using that as an excuse to carry on smoking. Stopping smoking isn't something that happens on its own. You do have to work on it. It is a life-changing project and I think a life-changing project warrants some space of its own.

Which brings me now to staying stopped. Stopped and staying stopped aren't two separate subjects. Every smoker stops every day, at night, or even frankly between cigarettes. Everyone dies a non-smoker, because unless you die with a cigarette in your mouth you can't know for sure that you would light another cigarette ever again. Interestingly, you could say you are only a smoker if you are actually smoking a cigarette. You might think this is logical argument gone mad but it isn't. After all, if you have ever stopped before you will know that people say if you smoke just one cigarette it means you have started again. It's nonsense of course but let's take it at face value for now. If one cigarette means you are a smoker, doesn't not smoking right now mean you are a non-smoker? It sounds crazy, even to me when I write it, but it's unassailably logical.

So how do you distinguish between being stopped and not being stopped, really? Well, unsurprisingly I shall be talking about that later so I'm not going into a lot of detail now, but the larger question is why is staying stopped so hard, and the answer is perhaps that people think they have started smoking again when they haven't, because smoking one cigarette, or even a whole pack, does not mean you have started smoking again.

It could, but it doesn't have to. Not if you don't want it to. So the question why is it hard to stay stopped is actually two questions:

- Why is it hard not to smoke a cigarette once you've stopped?

- Why is it hard not to go back to smoking once you've had a cigarette?

Some of the smokers who phone us, those who have been stopped before, say they were happy non-smokers and they were shocked when they started again. Others say they were never sure they were non-smokers. It was more like they were smokers who weren't smoking, which sounds daft but isn't. (Even stranger, we occasionally speak to someone who says they feel like a non-smoker who smokes. Figure that one out.)

The point is that being a non-smoker, as long as you were one before, is not that far removed from being a smoker. They say that someone who used to be alcoholic but isn't now is just one drink away from it, and it's reasonable to apply that idea to cigarettes. Once you've been a smoker, remember, you will always think like one, and even if you don't most of the time you can slip back into it very easily. When you become a smoker you cede control of your brain to the tobacco companies, for ever. I haven't smoked for years, and I know I never will again, but I also know that I used to. I cannot think like someone who has never smoked.

How about an analogy? Well, if you have been married and divorced, no future life, let alone future relationship, can exist as if that first marriage hadn't happened. We store in our brains the memory of everything that has ever happened to us. If you smoke 20 cigarettes a day and you've done that for twenty years that is 146,000 times you have lit up. Can you think of anything else you have done, consciously, 146,000 times in the past twenty years?

Now add to that the fact that each time you lit up you got a shot of the drug you are addicted to, and you get some idea of why, if we turn the question on its head, even if we don't talk in terms of it being hard to stay stopped it is easy to start again.

My point? Well, firstly that you should of course do everything in your power not to start again once you've stopped and you can be certain I shall have something useful to say about that later, but for now I'll tell you the big secret of not starting again.

It's not actually about not starting again at all. It's understanding that you might start again, because of what I've just been saying, but making a promise that if you ever do you will do something about it. I speak regularly with smokers who say they stopped once, or more than once, but they went back to it and now they've lost heart, lost faith in their ability ever to do it again.

That's not only terribly depressing but it's also silly.

Because if you've stopped before and started again, yes, you've proved that you can start again but you've also proved something else, something far more important.

That you can stop.

Fascinating Fact Number 3

The tobacco companies can almost certainly manufacture cigarettes that don't contain nicotine but they don't. Why not? Surely it would be better? No, there would be no point, because if tobacco didn't contain nicotine no-one would smoke it. They know why people smoke - to get the drug. Taking the nicotine out would simply render smoking completely pointless, and their market would vanish.

Use this space to make any comments or
note any reminders for yourself.

Tutorial Four

Changing attitudes - yours especially

It's a funny old world, which I expect you realise, but I'm talking particularly about smoking.

A lot of people in this country have some input to the issue of smoking. The government regulates it but it also taxes it, which means it has a financial interest in its continued use. Doctors are tasked with doing something about it but they have no training in addiction and in any case they haven't been told by the government to treat smoking as addiction or given anything to do that with.

The business world sees tobacco as a completely normal industry and makes no moral judgment about an industry that kills its customers. Retail business, even supermarket businesses like the Co-op which has higher ethical standards than most, sell tobacco as if that was alright.

Everyone's saying tut tut, tobacco, terrible stuff, but at the same time everyone's making money and shrugging their shoulders. They've got an attitude problem. You've got an attitude problem too, but you didn't get that attitude in isolation, you caught it from other people. Tobacco kills twelve hundred Americans each day but you see people smoking it in the street and you shrug your shoulders. Everyone is apparently saying it's alright, so how are you supposed to think differently?

I've probably mentioned it already but let's talk about this expression, giving up smoking. It's the wrong way to say it and it gives people the wrong attitude towards stopping. I would go as far as to say that there is a general attitude that it's a shame people have to stop smoking, wouldn't it be nice if they could just carry on? That attitude was expressed some time ago by a British government minister who said poor people shouldn't be harassed about their smoking because, bless them, it's the only pleasure they've got. Excuse me? Barmy or what? And these people, heaven help us, run the country.

If you are going to stop smoking there are two things you have to do in this department. You have to accept that other people are wrong and you might be the only sane person on the planet (I do) and you have to change your attitude. If you are going to go into this with the attitude that you wish you could carry on smoking but you can't so as much as you hate to do it you really must give it up, well then you are going to struggle. No you're not, you're going to fail.

In one way, you're in luck, because you're reading this Handbook, and by the time you've finished it I have some hope you will be thinking differently. Instead of thinking you can't cope with the stress of life without smoking you will know you can, and even if you can't it's not because you're not smoking.

Instead of thinking life won't be fun without cigarettes you will look forward to being free, to enjoying going to the pub and not having to go outside and smoke.

Instead of saying one won't hurt you will ask yourself why the hell you would smoke even one.

Instead of being afraid of stopping you will be afraid to carry on smoking.

Of course, you might not, and maybe now you're thinking oh no I won't, but look, if you're fighting it now you've just proved you've got the wrong attitude.

And now I come to a particular problem for smokers. Everyone keeps telling you to stop smoking, don't they? People keep having a go at you and you wish they wouldn't. You'll smoke if you want to. Columnists write in the papers about the 'smoking police' and the 'nanny state'. Oho, aren't they clever? No, they're just writing any old rubbish that sells papers and pays them a fee for the piece. You don't think journalists actually believe what they write, do you? They produce words for a living. It doesn't matter to them which words. If there's a new regulation about where people can smoke, they will just write a piece that feeds on the popular resentment about that regulation. If their piece has the effect of making smokers more determined to carry on smoking and that shortens their lives, do you think the writer is going to lose any sleep? I don't think so.

Hostility to a government that introduces more smoking regulations is completely self-defeating. They're not having a go at you. They don't care about you. Banning you from smoking in public places isn't for your benefit, it's for the benefit of non-smokers. Actually, even that's not the whole story because what it's really about is non-smokers suing employers and local authorities and even the government, bless them, for getting smoking-related diseases from passive smoking. That's all it is. You are not the target, so stop worrying about it.

And in any case, regulations about where you can and can't smoke have nothing whatever to do with stopping. A government that says such regulations will have the effect of reducing smoking are either lying or deluding themselves, both things governments do habitually. Why would anyone stop smoking just because they can't smoke in the pub? Alright, the more smoking is restricted the fewer cigarettes some people will smoke simply because of the difficulty, but to be honest the effect is fairly minimal. I know, because we talk to tobacconists, who are a lot more reliable as informants than health authorities who have a reason for making false claims because it justifies their budgets, and tobacconists don't see a reduction in sales.

My point for you though is that no-one is saying you have got to stop smoking. Why would I, someone who spends every waking minute helping people stop smoking, say that? Because like it or not it's true. If you are going to carry on smoking just because you think everyone is having a go at you, it's time to rethink that idea. There is only one person who matters - you.

You put up problems - you know, you won't know what to do with your hands, you won't be able to handle stress, you won't enjoy a drink, but these aren't real problems, they're excuses. There is no problem that you cannot overcome, but you need a major attitude overhaul first. You need to accept, right now, that you want to be a non-smoker and that there is no reason why you should not have what you want.

Now you may have noticed that you don't have the same attitude towards smoking, or stopping, as people who don't smoke. You suspect that anyone who doesn't smoke doesn't understand, and you are probably right. There is a brotherhood (sisterhood, whatever) of smokers, and they understand each other but other people don't. It's part of the persecution complex smokers have, thinking everyone is ganging up on them, but that's by the by, because I want to explain why the two groups, smokers and non-smokers, have such a different way of thinking about smoking.

Neither side is right, or wrong. OK, people who say you shouldn't smoke probably have a point, which gives them a right to think it but not necessarily the right to say it, but that's not what I want to talk about. I want to explain a very specific reason why you think about smoking the way you do.

You are going to be reading a lot, shortly, about the psychological dependence that the addiction to nicotine creates. That dependence can go very deep and change people's perceptions of smoking and the need to stop and also their ability to stop. That is what it's for. The tobacco companies need to change what we might call the correct way to think about smoking, which should be entirely negative, into a more positive way of thinking. They know that the addiction to nicotine changes the way you see the drug. They know that it is the addiction to nicotine that gives you the wrong (or what they call right) attitude not only to smoking, in that you see it as alright, but to stopping, which you see as not alright.

In other words, or fewer words, you can't think the right way about smoking and stopping because you are an addict. You can't expect to think the right way, because you are an addict. It's a wonderful trick. You are addicted so you can't think straight about becoming unaddicted, which is the tobacco companies' first line of defence against you stopping.

You begin to get the idea from the way I explain things that smoking is a war between you and the tobacco companies. I can't help it. When you've seen as many smokers as I have, and the regrets they have, it's an attitude you develop.

So, if you are going to stop smoking you are going to have to accept three things:

- You have the wrong attitude.
- That attitude was created by your addiction to nicotine.
- It is a deliberate tactic by the tobacco companies to keep your money coming in.

Now, what can you do about this? How can you take on the tobacco companies and win? How can you get back control of your life?

It's blindingly simple. The only person who is afraid to stop smoking is a smoker. Non-smokers aren't afraid, are they? Why? Because they aren't addicted, so they have control of the way they see tobacco. Therefore, love it or hate it, if you become a non-smoker you will start to see tobacco differently and you will suddenly find it was what you wanted all along. That you used to think the wrong way because you were being manipulated, but that is over, and you have won back your freedom.

Take on that challenge, even if right now you don't see it. After all, what do you have to lose? If you say to yourself I'm not a hundred percent sure I want to stop but I accept that's because tobacco is controlling me so I'll stop anyway and then decide if I want to start again, what do you have to lose?

It's scary, I know, but think about it. I like this idea so much I shall probably remind you of it later.

Case Study

Janice did our Phoenix Programme and in the clinic she didn't present as a difficult case. She left on a high, like most people do, and we put her down as more than likely to be successful.

She wasn't though. She stopped smoking for a week or so, but then she started again, and try as we might to get her to explain why, she couldn't. She stopped regularly, but she always started again, and every time there was a different reason - social, stress, boredom, whatever, the usual excuses, but none of it made a lot of sense. We held a case conference in the office and none of my colleagues could come up with an answer.

Janice stayed with the programme, which was good, because some smokers give up if it doesn't work the first time, which is intensely frustrating for us. We even got into a routine, where she would stop for a while and then phone to say she was smoking (not a lot, admittedly) and we would have a chat, about anything really, life, and she would stop again for a while. Her case notes said we couldn't see a way out of this.

And then it happened. Not because of anything we said or did but because she was ready to talk about it. When she was a teenager, she and her brother started smoking at the same time and they became partners in crime and even as young adults they often got together to smoke. It was their thing. Then her brother committed suicide. Now, she smoked to be near him. What could we do for her? Nothing, of course, This wasn't about smoking. And that's the point; it isn't always about smoking, it's sometimes about smoking becoming embedded in other life issues, and in a case like this clearly the patient needs to address those issues before they will stop smoking.

Although our counsellors are very good, they are specialist smoking cessation counsellors, and we are regularly reminded just how damaged some people are before they come to us, and these are issues we are not qualified to get into. On the other hand, I personally believe that even someone with serious psychological issues can stop smoking, and something interesting will happen when they do that. Their success will boost their self-worth, help them adopt a new attitude to themselves if you like, and in my experience that only ever helps people to live their lives better.

There's just one more thing I want to say on this subject. As you know, I spend my entire working life talking to smokers. It's hard work but someone's got to do it. And one thing that comes out in these consultations time and time again is people's inability, or refusal, I don't know which, to accept responsibility.

They say things like, oh I did such and such a programme, but it didn't work. Or I used that new drug and it didn't work. Well, excuse me, let's be quite clear about something here. Whether you smoke or not is up to one person and one person only - you. I know you don't like it but that doesn't stop it being true.

It's like saying I bought some new running shoes, really expensive they were, but I still didn't win the Marathon. No, well, I think you see where that comment might be going wrong. So why can't smokers see that blaming a product or programme when they fail to stop smoking might be a mistake? I say might, because on the other hand it might be completely right, they might have bought something that was just useless. On the other hand, they might have bought something that works for some people but didn't work for them. Does that mean it doesn't work? No, it means it didn't work. So why didn't it work for them? Probably because it was the wrong thing for them (you will be learning how to find the right solution in Part 2). Buying the wrong programme, or just taking any old prescription your GP gives you, is an abdication of responsibility and it leads to failure more often than not.

So one big change you are going to make right now is that you are no longer going to swallow pills blindly, or pay out silly money to therapists who promise you things they have no right to promise you. You are going to take responsibility for your own project to stop smoking. It involves quite a major change in attitude but it's worth it.

You have been warned. Just don't come crying to me if it all goes wrong and you haven't even done this one simple thing.

Now I want to come to something you may never have thought of. You have a relationship with tobacco. You have unthinkingly accepted that relationship and I think you might even have had some inkling that it is a relationship, because there have been times when it's been good and times when it has been bad. But smoking isn't something you just do. From now on, I want you to consider yourself to be in this relationship, and I want you to question whether it's a good one. I have known smokers leave a partner rather than stop smoking, so clearly this relationship goes pretty deep.

The point is that it's a relationship of abuse. And it's a classic abusive relationship, in which tobacco hurts you and at the same time it makes you afraid to leave it. If you are going to stop smoking (and you are), you are going to have to take control of this relationship. From now on, you need to see tobacco (not smoking) as your enemy, and yourself as its victim. You need a new attitude, don't you? You need to stand up for yourself.

Would you let anyone else treat you this way?

Rebellion

You would be amazed at the number of smokers we see who say not only that they started smoking as an act of rebellion, which is not surprising at all, but that they still smoke as an act of rebellion. And I'm talking about grown-ups here, bearing in mind that most smokers are in their thirties, minimum, before they come to us for help.

Sometimes they are rebelling against a partner who

doesn't want them to smoke, and that's a relationship problem not a smoking problem, but more often it's a way of saying I can still do what I want and no-one is going to force me to stop smoking so there.

Well I think we should give that idea a test for grown-upness. Exactly how adult is it to take a drug in the full and certain knowledge that it is hurting you, as a way of stating your individuality? Especially when millions of other people are doing it.

But that's not really the point. The point is that imagining you are smoking as a way of establishing your freedom to smoke is a complete nonsense. You're also free to leap off a motorway bridge, but strangely that's a freedom you accept as given without the need to prove it, and strangely too it's not a freedom that has a lot of value to you.

Yes, of course you are free to smoke. I am free to smoke. In that way we are the same. The difference between us is that I am also free to not smoke but you are so busy asserting your right to do it that you have missed the fact that you have given up your right to choose not to do it. By insisting on your freedom to use an addictive drug, you abdicate the freedom not to.

You are not rebelling when you smoke, you are conforming. You are doing what multinational tobacco companies, and your government, need you to do. Well done.

Rebellion is about asserting your rights as an individual. Buying an addictive drug means giving up those rights. It's not grown-up at all, it's infantile.

Smoking is drug taking

And now I want to make a statement that you should think about very carefully. Why do people smoke? Because they like the taste? Because it helps to relax them? Because it's a sociable thing to do? Why? All of the possible reasons you currently have in your mind are, during the course of this Handbook, thoroughly and conclusively proved incorrect. So the question remains, and must be answered, why do people smoke, why do you smoke?

Smoking is drug-taking. Whatever else you think it is, you are wrong, it is nothing more or less than drug taking. You may not like me saying this but accept it for two reasons:

- It is correct, and if you are going to remain in denial you will fail to stop smoking.

- Unless you adopt this attitude, you are refusing to change, and if you won't change, for its own sake even if you don't like what I'm saying, you are going to fail to stop smoking.

Stop blaming yourself

It's an interesting factor in smokers' motivation, or lack of it, that they blame themselves for the problem. This has the paradoxical effect of making them think well it's my own fault, I can't blame anyone else, so that's that. I'm not sure why people's belief that it's their own fault equates to being unable to stop smoking, but it does.

First of all it's not your fault that you smoke. Smoking is not, contrary to the popular myth, self-inflicted. If you started when you were a child, like most smokers, you were under the age of responsibility and you can blame the adult world for not protecting you from the drug. Once you tried it, you came under its control, so you can blame the authorities who allowed its sale. Once you were addicted, you became psychologically dependent. Alright, perhaps you should have been stronger, but you were what you were and in normal times that hasn't been a problem, has it? There is, then, a very strong case for not accepting the blame for your smoking.

But in any case, even if it WERE your fault, which it isn't but if it were, there is a serious error in believing that means that you will only stop smoking when you can get your head round it which isn't now because you're not ready, or whatever other reason you give, but as sure as eggs is eggs you can at least convince yourself that because it's all your fault you have to accept your hopelessness.

So two attitude changes are needed here. First, start blaming other people for the mess you're in and second, stop allowing yourself to feel a hopeless weakling.

A small suggestion

People get terribly worked up about stopping smoking, before they do it, while they're doing it, and even after they've done it. I have spoken with I don't know how many smokers in the process of stopping who feel trapped - they don't want to go forward because it hurts, but they don't want to go backward because they daren't. We always say the same thing to these people. We remind them, or inform them even, that the reason they feel so stressed about it is NOT because they are stopping smoking. This surprises them, and it probably surprises you.

You are stressed because you STARTED smoking. It is smoking that has done this to you, not stopping. If you had never started you wouldn't have to go through the process of stopping. Yes, you could forget the last section and blame yourself for starting, but that's the point - it isn't you, it's tobacco. If tobacco hadn't done this to you, you wouldn't be in this position. So the sooner you come off it the sooner you get back your self-respect. Then, because you have regained control, you can decide never to let tobacco do that to you again.

Fascinating Fact Number 4

Every time you stop smoking and start again it gets harder to stop again. The effect is more often than not psychological - you think you just can't face it again, but funnily enough even smokers whose memory of not smoking was great can't face it, so what is the reason?

It's because when you stop you go through withdrawal from nicotine and this sets a flag in your brain that watches out for any further attempt to stop and fights it. Naturally, the way it does this is to make you feel very negative about it. Don't be put off by this effect, but do decide that this time you won't make the same mistakes.

Use this space to make any comments or
note any reminders for yourself.

Tutorial Five

Addiction - what it is and how it works

Take a substance, say tobacco, which for the sake of this argument, no-one has ever used. Dream up some marketing campaign to get people not only to try it, but to convince them that, although it tastes revolting, they should keep using it until they can overcome their distaste. Add massive punitive taxation, and then persuade every user that their life would not be worth living without it, even if they are on benefits and have to go without food to get it. Then put a death threat on the pack.

The person who could do all this does not exist. Either millions of people are certifiably insane, or there is something in tobacco that forces them to continue using it.

There are very many learned societies that sit around and talk about addiction and publish terribly erudite papers on the subject but I'm going to be very rude now and say they don't understand it. How do I know?

Because no-one has ever been able to cure it.

(This is not actually true, because there was one doctor who, in a discovery of massive importance, did understand how addiction works, and proposed a really quite simple cure for it, which was proved to work, but there was no way the pharmaceutical companies could find to patent it and make a profit from it so it was quietly dropped. The National Smoking Cessation Institute was set up specifically to continue his work. Dr Mackarness taught a small group of doctors about the mechanisms of addiction and the Institute is the repository of that research. We have offered the information, free, to the nation but the Department of Health has turned it down because if it were brought to light the pharmaceutical companies would withdraw their funding for the NHS smoking cessation service, which is paid for by commercial sponsorship.)

I am now going to give you a layman's explanation of how addiction works. With this knowledge, you will know more, with all due respect to them, than most doctors.

First, let's have a look at some of the myths about addiction, because myths are terribly destructive things. People go around believing the wrong things and because of that they do all the wrong things in an attempt to solve the problem. So here, first of all, is what addiction is not.

Myth number 1
Addiction happens because you like something so much you can't stop using it

How can this possibly be true? Look at typical addictive

substances - tobacco, coffee and alcohol, for example. Take a child who has never had any of these and give them some. If the theory of lethal attraction is right, the child will want more straight away. In fact the first dose of any of these substances is unpleasant, even repellent. You may well remember that reaction yourself. I do. The child has to learn to like the taste of these things.

So the reason you are addicted to tobacco cannot possibly be because it's so good you can't stand the thought of not having it. You may well have developed a deep psychological dependence that tries to convince you that you do like the taste, but that is brainwashing and has nothing to do with what I'm talking about here, the physiological dependence on a substance. Just to be quite sure about this, now let's consider whether any substance could be so nice you would be prepared to die for it. 14 million Britons use tobacco. The pack has a death threat on it which, OK, you ignore, but even so you know it's there and you know it's true. The reason it has that threat on it is because every six minutes in this country one person dies prematurely from a disease caused by tobacco.

So you and 14 million other people know this but it's so nice, well, you'll just have to die rather than miss the enjoyment. I don't think so. Clearly, addiction has nothing whatever to do with pleasure.

Myth number 2
Some people are more addicted than others

This might be possible if the fatal attraction theory were valid - some people might be more fatally attracted than others. But it's not, so it isn't. Perhaps a heavy smoker is more addicted than a light smoker? Wrong again. Some people are light smokers in the week and they smoke more at the weekend, or in the evenings or when they are under great stress. Does that mean they are more addicted at those times? No, it's just plain silly.

How much you smoke has nothing to do with how addicted you are for two reasons. The first is that the amount you smoke is entirely a function of psychological triggers, and the second is that there are no degrees of addicted. You either are or you are not. It is a fundamental truism of the mechanics of addiction, and you will learn why that is shortly.

Myth number 3
Some people have an addictive personality

This might be possible if addiction were a psychological phenomenon, but it isn't, it's entirely physiological. It affects your personality because you become psychologically dependent on the delivery method for the drug, but it cannot happen the other way round. You can't have a personality that makes you addicted.

You can have a personality that makes you try a drug and expose yourself to becoming addicted, but that's different. You might have a dependent personality and you might think the difference between addiction and dependence is just a semantic one, and you would be right, without the just. Addiction and dependence are two quite separate things, which you are going to be learning about in detail, but I don't want to hear you saying one thing and meaning another because it's not helpful.

Myth number 4
Addiction doesn't matter when you stop smoking

Of course it doesn't. It doesn't matter when you try to come off heroin either. Really, what nonsense this is, and it's usually peddled by people who have a great theory about the psychology of drug taking and don't want the facts to get in the way.

Alright then, if addiction doesn't matter, why do you smoke? What is the fatal flaw in your character that forces you to use a drug that kills 300 Britons a day because you 'enjoy' it, or because it's just a 'habit', or because you like to smoke when you drink? This is a bit early to be claiming insanity.

Am I saying that addiction is the sole reason you smoke? No, or haven't you been paying attention? Addiction is the basis of all drug taking, but that addiction creates the psychological dependence on the delivery method for the drug. That's not what I'm talking about right now, so let's stick with the subject in hand.

If you don't believe me, here's some proof that addiction is what it's about. Herbal cigarettes cost about half what tobacco ones cost, but people don't smoke them. Well, excuse me, smoking is smoking (yes, I know they smell strange, but no stranger than tobacco to a non-addict). Why don't people smoke them if they are so cheap, especially people who haven't got much money? There is only one reason. Herbal cigarettes cannot deliver nicotine. Yes, they're smoking, but smoking is not the point. Without the drug, a cigarette is of no interest to a smoker. You smoke cigarettes to get a fix. It's that simple. Addiction isn't the only reason you haven't stopped smoking, but it is the only reason for the other reasons, if you see what I mean, which you will soon.

Myth number 5
You can't be addicted because you can go all night without smoking

And on a long-haul flight, and all day at work, so clearly you are not addicted. Sorry, but it means nothing.

It is not possible for the human body to absorb nicotine regularly and not be addicted, and by regularly I mean once every four days. That means one cigarette, or someone else's cigarette, because if you can smell the smoke you are getting the nicotine. This myth comes out of confusion over what addiction means. Being able to refrain from smoking for several hours is not, I'm afraid, a measure of whether you are addicted or not.

OK, so much for the myths. Now, you no longer believe the wrong things, and you would probably like to know exactly what addiction is and how it works. Ready for this?

What is the difference between addiction and dependence?

Let's get our terminology right first. People who are uneducated in this subject, and I include some medical people, use the words interchangeably, but that's them and you're you, so don't you do it.

Addiction refers to the physiological need for a substance, a need you are going to be reading about.

The addiction to nicotine, you might be surprised to hear, does not make you smoke. What it does do is give you withdrawal symptoms that make your brain compute a way to stop them, which happens to be smoking, and it does this over and over again until you believe you can't live your life without smoking. That stage is what is called psychological dependence, which means your brain believes it needs the drug to the extent that even if the drug stopped being needed your brain would refuse to believe it. It's complicated but don't worry because I'll be explaining all of that too in a lot more detail later.

There are some people, journalists, doctors, you know, people who think they know but don't, who refer to something they call psychological addiction. This is, of course, an oxymoron. Addiction cannot be psychological by definition. An example of this error is saying someone is addicted to gambling or sex. Not possible. Dependent on, yes, but addicted to, no. Does it matter if people use the wrong words? For Heaven's sake, of course it does.

How addiction works

Do you remember the first time you ever smoked? Or the first time you smoked again after you had been stopped? What was it like? Almost all smokers remember (I do) that it was bad. It will have tasted bad and perhaps made you nauseous and/or dizzy.

Why do you think it has this effect? Because it's poisonous. Tobacco smoke contains 4865 different poisonous substances. It is the most toxic thing you will ever put into your body. So, if it's that poisonous how would you expect your body to react? Not unnaturally, your body will ask you not to do it. It's quite normal and it's part of your immune defence. If you absorb a poison, your immune system gives you symptoms which are signals to your brain not to do it. If you ignore those signals you run a severe risk of illness and death.

It's like putting your hand on the hotplate of your cooker. Your body reacts with pain to get you to stop, and you do. Smokers though do just the opposite. They react with pain so they think mm, that was horrible, I'd better do it again.

Why would anyone be that daft? Because they are under psychological pressure to learn how to smoke. Your friends didn't cough and splutter or go green or throw up, so you wanted to be like them and so you smoked another and another and what you did was to learn to smoke.

Now, learning to smoke actually means doing something very specific in medical terms. It means teaching your immune system to stop telling you that tobacco smoke is poisonous. It's a good trick and it's incredibly dangerous, because your immune system being unable to tell you that it's poisonous doesn't stop it being poisonous. It's like your nerves being disconnected in your hand so you don't feel the heat when you burn it.

When you learned to smoke, all you did was to stop your body protecting itself from being poisoned by tobacco. That's why tobacco kills, because it has carte blanche to poison you without you knowing it.

So far so good, or possibly bad, but what happens then? Well, I have to admit that no-one understands this mechanism completely, for the rather bizarre reason that there is no government funding for research into it. The only research we are aware of is being done by us, and you might imagine we don't have a lot of money, so what we can do is limited. The drug companies, of course, don't do the research because there would be no point. It wouldn't help them to develop new drugs.

Back to the plot. What we do know is that the immune system does something very strange when it is forced to accept poisons. It goes into reverse. If you insist on poisoning yourself, your immune system thinks that's what you want to do and it says alright, if you insist, and throws itself completely into reverse mode and now, instead of trying to protect you from poisoning yourself it tries to protect you from stopping.

If you want to know more about it, here goes, but if you don't skip this next paragraph.

The doctor who did the original work, Dr Richard Mackarness, wasn't actually looking at addiction at all. He was an allergy specialist. He developed some research work that was done in the US that enabled him to produce an antidote for any known allergen. It was a great success, even though the NHS in the UK wouldn't back his work, and he wrote books about it and over the years became rather famous in his specialised field. Then he got to thinking, and what he thought was that if he could cure allergy, which he could, he might be able to cure addiction. Why? Well, think about it. What does allergy mean? In simple terms, that your immune system mistakenly thinks a substance is a poison and gives you the symptoms of poisoning when you ingest it. Sound familiar? When you inhale tobacco smoke and force your immune system to adapt to it, it does exactly what it does in an allergic reaction, only now instead of reacting when you have it it reacts when you don't have it. Allergy doctors call this masked allergy. Your immune system only reacts to tobacco smoke when it doesn't get it. This was a breakthrough on a level with Pasteur, and I say that unashamedly. What Dr Mackarness had done by discovering how to switch off an addictive reaction was simply to expose what the mechanism is that causes that reaction.

That he didn't win international acclaim, if not a Nobel Prize for medicine, is purely a function of commercial imperatives and is a disgrace, but don't get me started on that, which I will because Dr Mackarness saved my life and before he died I made a promise, that I would not let his work die with him. It has cost me in excess of a million pounds so far, but look, a promise is a promise. OK, now you know I'm serious about this.

So what you've got is an immune system that has been trained not only to accept poisons without producing symptoms, but in fact that will produce symptoms when it doesn't see the poisons. That, in a nutshell, is the sum total of how addiction works. Withdrawal symptoms are signals from your immune system to your brain to look for the poisons it is adapted to.

The same, by the way, applies to all addiction, not only tobacco.

How do you know if you are addicted to nicotine?

Well, you are, but you want some proof, don't you?

- Do you have an urge to smoke as soon as you

wake up?

- If you haven't smoked for a couple of hours, does a cigarette give you an immediate feeling of relief?

- Do you use more cigarettes in the first hour of the day than at any other time?

- When you are in a non-smoking environment, do you look forward to getting out so you can light up?

- Do you make sure you won't run out of cigarettes?

- When you haven't smoked for several hours, do you experience mild symptoms such as headache, stomach cramps, sweats?

Not one of these can be attributed to any of the psychological problems you think you've got about stopping. You don't want to smoke when you wake up out of habit, you want to smoke because you need nicotine. The relief you feel when you smoke might be interpreted as pleasure (more about that later) but it isn't, it's just relief because you're getting a fix. You don't make sure you don't run out of cigarettes in case you might be stressed and need to smoke, you do it because you are addicted. You get the idea, I expect.

If any of the above applies to you you are addicted, but in any case it's certain that you are addicted, if you smoke at least four cigarettes a day.

Why?

The Addiction Threshold

The human body needs to see nicotine about four times a day to avoid going into withdrawal. People who smoke very lightly tend to do so spread over the day, for this reason (without of course realising what they are doing). This is because nicotine is lost very quickly and must be replaced every few hours. You might be wondering how you lose nicotine, since I mention it.

Well, in a number of ways, the first one being the way you took it in, through the mouth. You know you can see tobacco smoke coming out of your mouth when you smoke. That smoke contains nicotine. After you put the cigarette out the nicotine continues to come out of your mouth with each breath, even if you can no longer see smoke.

The second most important way you lose it is through the skin. Your skin is your largest cleansing organ. Every pore can ooze nicotine (and the other toxins in tobacco, which is why you smell) and does so to help you get rid of it. Then, finally, you excrete it as waste through the bladder and the bowel. So you lose it quickly but steadily, and after enough has been lost you start to need more.

So the threshold, below which you will go into withdrawal, is about four cigarettes a day, depending on a number of factors like your bodyweight, the amount of exercise you take and your diet, especially your fluid intake.

We regularly get calls from people who say they have

been heavy smokers but they've managed to cut right down, and they are always surprised when we say no, no, don't tell me, about four a day? Any heavy smoker can cut down to that level with the right motivation and maybe some practical help, but going below the threshold challenges your addiction and that is harder.

You will find, when you come to do the projects in Part 2, that this fact is going to help you to stop smoking.

Maintaining the addiction

Although you need about four cigarettes or so each day to avoid withdrawal symptoms, the addiction is not finally lost until there is no longer any nicotine in your body. That takes about four days, variable again for the same reasons as above. This is why some people are extremely light smokers, and why some are what they call social smokers. They tend to say oh I can take it or leave it, I only smoke when I go to the pub, but in most cases they are going to the pub at least twice a week, and while they don't like to be told they are addicted, as if that's some kind of insult, technically they are.

Passive smoking

There is enough nicotine in someone else's smoke to keep you addicted. Some people don't even need to smoke. They just keep breathing smoke from other people's cigarettes and they can avoid withdrawal symptoms.

We once had a woman asking us for help. She said that every time she stopped smoking her daughter's behaviour changed. Was it just that she was stressed and she thought it changed?

Unlikely, but we tested the daughter at the same time as her mother and, yes, she was addicted. She was 11 years old. She had never smoked a cigarette, but she was addicted to the nicotine she had been absorbing from her mother's smoking. We had to treat her at the same time as her mother to get round the problem.

Naturally, then, when you stop smoking it is important to avoid smoky places, which in any case is easy enough to do these days, but it also means, if you have a smoking person in your household, that they cannot smoke in the same room as you. This is not an option. I don't care what you have to say to them, but this is non-negotiable. They might not like it, and they might threaten to leave you but look, my thing is smoking not relationships, so I can't help you there.

Tomatoes

Ah, tomatoes again. Yes folks, the humble tomato is the only food that can keep you addicted to nicotine. You'll be reading about this problem, and what you need to do about it, in Tutorial 10.

Withdrawal symptoms are natural

You probably associate the word withdrawal with addiction, and perhaps you believe this concerns other people but not you. Withdrawal symptoms are a completely natural human function. If you didn't have them you would die. Everyone has withdrawal symptoms every day, from two substances.

How do you know when your body needs fluids? You get thirsty. How do you know when your body needs nutrition? That's right, you get hungry, usually manifesting as a rumbling tummy, getting worse if you don't eat. Eventually, if you still don't eat, you get more serious symptoms like weakness, faintness and confusion.

All of these are symptoms your body uses to make your brain respond to a physical need. When your brain recognises hunger signals, it institutes the process of eating. When you have eaten, you feel satisfied and the withdrawal symptoms stop - until you need more food.

If all of this sounds much like smoking, that's because it is. When you become addicted, to any drug, you use this existing withdrawal mechanism as the way you know you need feeding. The existence of this natural mechanism is one of the reasons it is so easy to become addicted to nicotine.

People often say they don't have withdrawal symptoms when they stop smoking. Well, that might or might not be true, because there is one particular symptom that many people fail to interpret as such. Fair enough, headaches, sweating, shaking, these are withdrawal symptoms that are common to many drugs. Coffee addicts experience them, for example. But there is an important difference between the addiction to nicotine and the addiction to almost every other substance people abuse.

It is used more often. There are very few people who smoke twenty cigarettes a day and take any other drug that often as well, even coffee. And what is the point to this? The point is how taking a drug that often affects your brain. You see, every time you put a cigarette out you go into what we call subliminal nicotine deprivation, which means the nicotine level drops without you noticing it - yet.

Long before you can possibly experience conscious withdrawal symptoms your body is already sending signals to your brain that you are withdrawing. And the brain, bless it, doesn't want you to have withdrawal symptoms so it tells you to light a cigarette before they can happen.

Therefore the craving/desire for a cigarette is itself a withdrawal symptom. Believe me, even if you think you have never experienced withdrawal symptoms you have, just before you lit the next cigarette, because what made you light it was the fact that you were in withdrawal from the last one.

(In fact 'wanting' to smoke is proof that you are addicted to nicotine. If you ever 'want' to smoke, which of course you do, regularly, this means you are addicted, which means if you are going to succeed at stopping smoking you are going to have to address the fundamental problem.)

Now you know how addiction works let's look, in the next tutorial, at how and why it is responsible for your psychological dependence on smoking.

Fascinating Fact Number 5

Quite a few cannabis smokers can't or won't stop using it not because they are addicted to the cannabis but because they roll their joints with tobacco and they have become addicted to nicotine.

When they come to stop smoking they will need to choose whether to continue smoking cannabis or not. If they do want to, they will either have to smoke it some other way, or to roll a joint buy some Honeyrose herbal smoking mixture (from a health food shop) and use that instead of tobacco. And then they must never accept a joint someone else has rolled but always carry the smoking mixture with them.

Use this space to make any comments or note any reminders for yourself.

Tutorial Six

Psychological dependence, what it is and what it does to you

Dependence on smoking keeps people smoking in three ways:

- It stops them trying to stop.
- It stops them succeeding when they try.
- It makes them go back when they have stopped.

Being dependent on something is not necessarily a bad thing. Dependence is what makes us form relationships and have families. The interdependency involved in these relationships is completely normal.

You have learned why and how you came to be addicted to nicotine, and now it's time to understand how that makes you dependent on smoking cigarettes and why this is a bad thing. In a nutshell it's a bad thing because being dependent on smoking is a terrible contradiction. It's not the comforting dependence that two people have when they love each other, it's the dependence one person has for another person who abuses them. Tobacco involves a love-hate relationship - you love it and it hates you. The function of tobacco is very simple. It is to make you and keep you dependent for the profit of others. It confers no benefit on the user and makes no claim to do so. It is, in fact, the only product sold legally on the planet that does this. Without the dependence of the users, the manufacturers would simply stop operating.

It is not, clearly, a normal relationship in the world of business. A company that knowingly sold a product that killed a consumer, I mean A consumer, not 300 a day in the UK alone, would be charged with corporate manslaughter. Tobacco companies not only kill their customers but they even tell them they're going to do it. That, by the way, is a very clever trick on the part of the government. The health warning on the pack enables the pushers to claim that they warned you but you still bought it out of free choice, so you can't have a claim against them in the courts. The government, bless them, by making health warnings on cigarette packs compulsory, did the manufacturers a huge favour in protecting them from their victims. They're not as daft as they look, are they?

And the real issue here is that the pushers say you have a free choice about using the product. It's like a man who abuses his wife saying she can always leave him, knowing she's too scared to do that. Because dependence is actually very very serious. It means much more than you might think. It means that tobacco has control of you. A lot of smokers say they know this but actually even they, the honest ones, don't realise how serious that control is. Because, obviously, if they did, they would do something about it. The sad thing is that a lot of smokers, the young ones, have no idea what's being done to them, that they are selling their souls to the tobacco companies. They might think they are rebelling by smoking when everyone tells them not to, but actually they're doing exactly the opposite, they're doing precisely what a group of multinational corporations want them to do.

A definition of dependence

I defined addiction in the last tutorial as a physiological need in the body for a poison that it was forced to adapt to, and I stressed, in case you have already forgotten, as if I would let you, that the addiction cannot be psychological. In other words, it can't be in your mind.

A simple definition of psychological dependence is that it is everything else. It encompasses every reason you can't stop smoking, other than your addiction to nicotine.

I'll come in a moment to exactly what that entails, but I want to emphasise before I go any further that you could not become psychologically dependent on smoking if smoking didn't give you nicotine. Try to imagine a heroin user claiming they love taking heroin because they have a thing about needles. Needles are the delivery method for the drug. They know that and you know it. But when it comes to smoking that knowledge gets reversed. Smokers imagine that what they love is the act of smoking, the lighting of a cigarette and inhaling the product of combustion of tobacco, the gases and tar going down their throat and into their lungs.

Psychological dependence produces what psychologists call cognitive dissonance, which means as far as we are concerned here that you know something is not true but you need it to be true so you make yourself believe it.

You know you don't have a valid argument for why you smoke so you invent one, the main ones being that you are stressed or that you enjoy it. In this Handbook I comprehensively destroy the possibility of either of those beliefs being true, but such is the grip that the addiction to nicotine has on your brain that you will read what I say, nod and say to yourself oh yes, he's quite right of course, and then you will look for a way to ignore it.

When I talk about nicotine turning your brain to mush, this is more or less what I mean. What can you do about that? Well, you have already started doing something about it, because you are reading this and absorbing what I'm saying and you are beginning to think it's important to stop tobacco controlling your brain. I hope.

Why dependence matters

Being dependent on smoking matters because it stops you being able to make rational judgments. It makes you believe things that are not true. For example:

- That you enjoy smoking and will miss it too much to stop.
- That smoking helps you to be less stressed.
- That it's just a habit.

- That you're not even sure you want to stop.

Well, I've already explained about how smoking reduces your motivation to stop smoking and you will be relieved to know I don't intend to go through all that again. The myths that smoking relieves stress, that you enjoy it, and that it's just a habit, are big issues, so I'm afraid they get lessons all to themselves.

Look, you've got to believe this stuff, and if I have to spell it out for you then frankly I've probably got more stamina for this than you have and I'll do it.

Seriously, if you take all this on board, you are never going to believe the wrong things again, and then, miraculously, you will have started to break the psychological dependence you have on smoking and then you will be more likely to stop smoking and that, if you remember, is the point of the Handbook.

Now I'm going to use a word you might not like. It's a word that encapsulates all the emotions involved in being dependent on smoking, that stops smokers sorting out the mess, coming to terms with what's happening to them and doing something about it. It's exactly the same thing that prevents a woman whose husband beats her from leaving him. It's what all abused people have.

It's fear.

The fear of stopping smoking

Fear is what makes people buy national lottery tickets. It's not the thought that they might win that makes them do it but the fear that someone else will. The sellers understand this, and it's part of their advertising. It could be you, but if you don't gamble (or 'play' as they call it) someone else will get all this lovely money that should be yours.

Fear is why drivers drop down to the speed limit when they reach a speed camera. They're not interested in obeying the law, they're just afraid of getting caught breaking it. I'm not being priggish when I say this, I'm just making a point. Fear is one of the most powerful motivating emotions a human will ever have. It is, for an industry that has a product to sell, an emotion they cannot afford to ignore. Fear is what keeps people smoking. And that brings me nicely back to my statement at the start of this tutorial, that there are three ways dependence works.

Case study

This is actually two case studies which illustrate fear.

Maureen was a woman in her sixties, very strong both physically (she was an ex-Olympic swimmer) and emotionally. Her husband attended the clinic with her, not as a patient but just to support her, which we approve of.

Before we had gone too long into the appointment a ghastly look came over Maureen's face and she got up from her seat. Before we had time to realise what was happening, she had crumpled onto the floor in the corner of the consulting room. She was shaking violently and crying. Her husband was, not surprisingly, highly alarmed. It was fear of going through with it. The nurse gave her a dose of Argentum Nitricum (a homeopathic remedy we sometimes use for fear) and helped her to do some breathing exercises, and in due course she calmed down and completed the session. She went on to stop smoking, but it was an eye-opener for her husband, who saw her as a swimming champion but had never known how afraid she was of stopping smoking. It was a bit of an eye-opener for us too.

Barry came to the clinic with his sister. Half-way through the session, after the nurse had given him his first dose of the neutrogen, he stood up and said he refused to continue, and he left the room very aggressively. His sister was acutely embarrassed but continued with her treatment. That afternoon, when we were in the next session with more patients, she knocked on the door of the clinic. Her brother had sent her, with his payment, and asked if he could have his neutrogen. He was too embarrassed to come himself, but they had sat in a pub over the road having lunch, and he realised that he didn't feel like smoking. The only thing that could overcome his fear of failure was seeing his own success. A week later his sister rang to request a repeat prescription for him, because he was still embarrassed, but was still not smoking.

Fear makes people do strange things, including refusing help from the very people who can make the fear go away.

Dependence stops you trying to stop

It does this through the mechanism of fear. We've already looked at the belief a lot of smokers have that they don't want to stop, contradicted by their admission that they regret ever starting, so clearly something is blocking their understanding that they do want to stop. That something is fear.

There are two fears all smokers have:

- The fear of failure.

- The fear of success.

It's a common human characteristic not to try something that you think you might fail at. It's more common among men, and I'm allowed to say that because I am one, because we don't want our pride dented by failure. We would rather not try than be shown up, even if it's only to ourselves.

The sad thing is that the fear of failing to stop smoking actually guarantees that you will fail, because you don't even try. This is much more common than you might think. Right now there are thousands of smokers out there who won't try to stop in case they fail, thus guaranteeing failure. It's crazy, isn't it? It's one of the very cunning ways all drugs have to keep people on them.

But by far the bigger problem is the fear of success. A lot of smokers who come to us are puzzled by this expression, so let me explain it. It means you are afraid that if you try to stop smoking you might succeed, despite the belief that that is exactly what you want, because you can't imagine living the rest of your life without smoking.

There, I've said it, and it's the big one. You can't imagine living the rest of your life without smoking. I know, I said that just now, but I wanted you to read it again. If you think this applies to you, read on. If not, you think I'm going to say skip the next bit but I'm not, I'm going to say if you don't think you are afraid of succeeding you are almost certainly deluding yourself. I say almost certainly because we do sometimes meet a smoker in our clinics who is genuinely not afraid of succeeding but I can tell you they are pretty rare. People think they want to stop smoking, but actually they are trying to carry themselves forward with that enthusiasm but it doesn't make any difference because at some point the fear will come back and bite them.

You think I'm making too much of this, don't you? Alright, let me ask you something. Have you helped tens of thousands of people to stop smoking? No? Well, in that case you are just going to have to assume I might know more about this than you do. I'm telling you, the vast majority of people smoking right now refuse even to contemplate stopping, and it's because of this fear. Why would anyone say anything as barmy as I want to carry on using this product that gives people cancer because I enjoy it? Come on. It's not remotely rational and they know it and so do you. So what makes them say it? The addiction? No, although as you know it's what made all this possible. It's because they believe the unbelievable. Tobacco rules you by tyranny. It is killing you and you know that and it knows you know but it also knows you won't come off it because you don't think your life would be worth living without it.

It is the completely irrational belief that they couldn't live without it that keeps most people smoking, and stops them even trying to stop. And there is an interesting reason why this is such a problem for so many people, something you may not have thought of.

If you have never managed to stop smoking, and let's

say you started when you were sixteen, which is pretty typical, you have never been an adult who doesn't smoke. You don't know what it's like to be an adult who doesn't smoke. And all humans have a fear of new experiences. They imagine the worst and avoid the experience if possible. You will avoid stopping smoking for many reasons, but one of them is simply that you have never done it. The fear of the unknown is a powerful disincentive and, if you have never stopped smoking before, you have it.

The funny thing is that all around you are people who don't smoke, people who used to and have stopped, and that should prove to you that life without smoking is amazingly similar to life with smoking. But it doesn't.

Dependence stops people successfully stopping

As you read this think how many people are currently trying to stop smoking. I don't know how many it is but it's a lot, let's say tens of thousands in the UK alone.

Based on studies published in the Lancet (of smokers on nicotine replacement products), more than 80 percent of those people will fail in the short term.

Now there are masses of reasons why people fail, and you've read about most of them in this Handbook already and actually there are more to come. But there is an overriding reason why people fail. They are afraid to succeed, so they sabotage themselves. You don't believe me? I'll give you an example.

A patient in our Phoenix Programme came to the clinic and went off a non-smoker. So far so good. He didn't smoke for a few days and then he rang to say he had been to a party and smoked. Now excuse me but if you know that at a party you are going to drink, quite a lot, and you know there are going to be people there who smoke and you know they are not likely to be exactly supportive of your attempt to stop, why the hell would you even go?

Oh, he said, it was already arranged. Yes well, my death is already arranged but I don't go out looking for it. Well, he added, I didn't want do disappoint my girlfriend. Really? Why not? Isn't she going to be more disappointed that you carry on smoking than that she misses one little party? Oh well, look, I should be able to go and enjoy a party, shouldn't I? I mean, it's not fair if I can't do that.

No, it's not, but boo hoo for you. It might, and here I may be going out on a limb but bear with me, be time to grow up, don't you think? Actually, I didn't say this, I just thought it.

Sabotage, I'm afraid, that's what it was. He could have kept himself out of harm's way but he did the opposite, he deliberately put himself in harm's way, he deliberately made it likely that he would smoke. Why would he do that? Why would someone who has decided to stop smoking, and paid let's face it good money to join a programme, wilfully wreck it all? The answer is, and you're probably ahead of me here, that he was afraid to succeed. (Don't worry about him, by the way, we got him through in the end, once he understood what he was doing and why.)

People regularly say to us, when they discuss their previous attempts to stop, before coming to us, that they reckon the reason they failed was because they didn't try hard enough, they weren't serious about it, it was the wrong time to try. They are almost entirely right. What they haven't understood is why all of these things. It's never going to be the right time to stop smoking, so frankly it might as well be now. It's only the wrong time because you don't know how to do it. When you do know how to do it, when you understand the issues, it will be the right time.

Now let me give you an example of someone who did the opposite. She was a journalist, doing the Phoenix Programme for a newspaper article she was writing about it. We reckoned she wasn't serious about stopping smoking, that she would write the piece and then forget all about it, but we underestimated her.

She called on day two of the programme (a requirement of all patients) and said that while she had been at the clinic her father had had a stroke. She learned about it when she left, and rushed to the hospital. Now, you know as well as I do that most people would say oh well this is certainly the wrong time to stop smoking but no, she said she didn't smoke. She had taken on board the correct belief that smoking was not going to help her or her father. We were impressed.

She rang a few days later and told us her father had died. We said the appropriate things and then asked did that mean she had started smoking again? Oh no, she said, I came to you the day he had the stroke. My not smoking will be dedicated to his memory. If we were impressed before, what do you think we felt now? It was simply brilliant. She could so easily have used her father's death as an excuse to fail, but instead she used it as a reason to succeed. Sometimes, not often but sometimes,

I am left in awe of the nobility of the human mind.

Dependence makes people start again

Once a smoker, always someone who used to be a smoker. It might sound a bit tedious but don't ever forget it. There's an entire tutorial later about not starting again once you've stopped, for obvious reasons, on account of it being a terribly important lesson to learn, but for now you need to understand that the fear that made it hard to face stopping, and the same fear that tried to prevent you succeeding, stays with you for the rest of your life. Alright, it gets less and less, but it never gives up hope that one day you will fall for it. It's a paradox, but the fear of never smoking again can come back and bite you years after you have stopped and found out that not smoking really is better than smoking. I ask you, how bizarre is that?

The majority of people who stop smoking start again, perhaps more than once. In fact you might say that it takes most people more than one attempt to succeed permanently, like it takes most people more than one attempt to pass a driving test (and why shouldn't it?). Once you have stopped smoking, you will use almost any excuse to start again, because you have retained the fear of success. You have succeeded, but you never quite believe it, and that, in short, is why so many people start again. The first bit of stress that comes along will make them start again, and that will prove to them that they couldn't stop smoking.

Even though they did.

And finally, it's worth reminding you that all of this fear

comes not because you've got to stop smoking at all. It comes because you STARTED smoking. Think about it.

When you start smoking you sell your soul to the devil. You allow tobacco to take over your brain, for ever. The job of tobacco is to control you, and you allow it to do that. It is the closest I can think of in the world of humans to turkeys voting for Christmas.

This lesson is so critical to you, I am going to summarise here what you must always remember:

- It says on the pack that it's going to kill you.
- Therefore, it must be true that, since you continue to smoke, smoking is controlling the way you think about smoking.
- If you continue to do it, it will continue to control the way you think about it, and you lose.
- If you stop doing it, you will regain control of the way you think about it, and you win.

Fascinating Fact Number 6

You don't actually need to inhale cigarette smoke to get nicotine. Think about nicotine replacement products. The patch squirts nicotine through your skin. The NRPs you use by mouth all squirt it through the lining of your mouth. And that's how you get it when you smoke - through the lining of your mouth. It's why cigar and pipe smokers, who don't inhale, are as addicted as cigarette smokers.

Why is it that cigarette smokers tend to get cancer of the lungs, while pipe and cigar smokers tend to get cancer of the mouth and throat? It's because the latter don't inhale the smoke. Some famous people, including Sigmund Freud and King George VI, were cigar smokers and had cancer of the mouth which contributed to their death.

Use this space to make any comments or
note any reminders for yourself.

Tutorial Seven

Habit, what it isn't, and why it doesn't matter

Here is a completely typical discussion with someone calling us about one of the Institute's programmes:

'So, what's the problem, why can't you stop?'

'Dunno. Just a habit, I guess.'

'Really?'

'Uhuh.'

'Alright. Would you like some help with that?'

'Pardon?'

'Would you like me to tell you how to overcome the problem of your habit so that you can stop smoking?'

'Um, will it cost anything?'

'Nope, it's our gift to you.'

'Oh. OK then.'

'Right, well first let's define what we mean by habit. Would you agree with me that what you mean is that you tend to smoke in certain situations, like with a drink, or a cup of coffee, or after a meal, or when you've finished a job, or when you get in the car after work, or when you're going to make a long phone call?'

'I suppose.'

'Yes or no?'

'Yes.'

'Are you smoking now?'

'Um, yes.'

'Good. Now, would you also agree that you smoke at all of those times habitually because you've got cigarettes with you all the time and it's easy to pick one up and light it without thinking?'

'Can I think about that?'

'Yes.'

'Well, yes.'

'Excellent.'

'Is it?'

'Yes. You have now resolved the reason you can't stop smoking.'

'I have?'

'Yes. You can't stop smoking, you say, because of the habit. And the habit is a problem because you've always got cigarettes with you. So don't have them with you. Don't buy cigarettes. You have now stopped smoking. Congratulations.'

'But...'

'Yes?'

'Aha, but if I didn't have them I would go out and buy some.'

'I know you would. But why?'

'Because I want them.'

'Why?'

'Well, I can't stop smoking, obviously.'

Dealing with smokers all day can start to get on your nerves sometimes. It takes a strong constitution. But it's moments like these that make it all worthwhile.

To continue:

'Thank you for saying that. You can't stop smoking so you buy cigarettes, and then because you've bought them you've got them and because you've got them you smoke them. Habitually. But it wasn't the habit that made you buy them in the first place, was it?'

'Well, no.'

'No, something else made you buy them, and that something is what we call addiction. Because you are addicted to nicotine you buy cigarettes and smoke them habitually. Resolve the right problem, the addiction, and the habit will vanish.'

It's completely irrefutable logic. There has never been an argument against it. Alright, smokers don't like it sometimes, but hey, we can't always do what they want. We're here to stop them smoking, not to be nice to them.

Habit does not stop you stopping smoking. End of story.

Except that I can't resist the temptation to say some more things about it, so it's not the end of this tutorial.

Habit is an odd word to use in connection with drug taking, don't you think? My dictionary defines it as, 'a behavioural pattern that has a degree of automatism'. That's it. Nothing about drugs. And yet it's the word of choice in connection with drug-taking. First of all, drug-taking has nothing to do with behaviour. Smoking has something to do with behaviour, yes, but that's the act of smoking itself, by which I mean lighting a cigarette, sticking it in your mouth and sucking on it.

But the reason you do that is not because you forget NOT to do it. You don't light cigarettes just because, well, it's a habit, you light them because they give you a fix.

OK, OK, I know what you're thinking, that there are lots of cigarettes you light out of habit and nothing more and yes, alright, if you absolutely insist, I will concede that point. Enjoy the moment, because I don't concede much, and anyway I'm still going to argue. If you are a smoker, a lot of the cigarettes you smoke are for no other reason than habit. There I said it. BUT, and I do mean but in capital letters, it's because you're a smoker that you do that. I'm not interested in why you smoke any given cigarette, say after work or with a drink. Really, I'm just not interested. What I'm interested in is why you are a smoker.

Why you are a smoker is everything, isn't it? Why you are a smoker is why you can't stop, after all. If you knew why you are a smoker you would be able to stop being a smoker, wouldn't you? And you are not, I repeat not, a smoker because you are in the habit of lighting a cigarette when you put the kettle on.

You are a smoker first because you are addicted to nicotine and second because that addiction has created the belief in your mind that you can't break the habit of smoking, when of course there's no connection.

And if you're still not sure (although how that would be possible I don't know) try this. Write down a list of all your habits. If some of them aren't very nice, do this in private. Now tick any of those habits that you would have serious difficulty breaking, if, say, your GP told you it was threatening your life. My guess is you won't be ticking anything other than smoking. Now go back to the list and tick any of your habits that happen to involve drugs. My guess now is that you've got one word, smoking, with two ticks against it.

The point of the exercise? Well, do I need to spell it out? Don't you find it just a tiny bit interesting that the only habit you can't break is the one where you take an addictive drug? Could it possibly be that what you think is habit is in fact the drug itself, not the habit at all? I'll give you a clue. The answer is yes.

You want more proof? Good grief, are you that sceptical? Alright, here goes.

Let's say you smoke 25 a day. Now let's compare the habit of smoking, in purely numerical terms (because the more you do something the more like a habit it seems, of course), with the other things you do in a typical day habitually.

Having done that, now let's multiply it all by the number of years you have smoked, and for the sake of this exercise I am going to say that's 25 years.

The list below might not apply to you but I think you will agree it's fairly exhaustive.

cups of tea/coffee	46,625	cigarettes	228,125
meals	27,375		
go to bed	9,125		
get up	9,125		
go to work	5,500		
feed the cat	18,250		
brush your teeth	18,250		
blow your nose	36,500		
wash the car	675		
Total	171,425		228,125

The chart shows that smoking is a habit like no other. Just look at the numbers. When you add up all those habitual things you do they still don't come to the same as the number of times you smoke. Is it any wonder people can't stop smoking?

On the other hand, let's take just one of the items on the list, feeding the cat. OK, I want you to imagine how you might break that particular habit. Yes, that's right, you could get rid of the cat. I'm not suggesting you do that really. I have two cats and I'd rather chuck my wife out than them, but seriously, if I suddenly developed a major allergy to them would I have a choice? However extreme, there is a way to break the habit of feeding them. If we don't have cats, we can't feed them. It's a terribly simple solution to the habit, don't you agree?

Similarly, if you didn't need to smoke and you therefore didn't buy cigarettes, the habit would be very simple to overcome.

Now, I think I've done this subject to death, so there's no more. If you don't believe me now you never will.

Association

Sorry, one more thing. You might well be in the habit of smoking in certain situations, as I've already said, like for example when you have a drink. But habit, as it happens, isn't exactly the right word for this.

You associate smoking with drinking, so when you drink you smoke, and in the long term you come to believe you can't do one without the other. Of course, you can, but you don't think you can so you don't.

Breaking the association is really hard. Remembering not to smoke when you have a drink, or make a long phone call, or finish work, is terribly difficult. Unless of course you are no longer addicted and therefore you don't have cigarettes with you and so no matter how much you associate that situation with smoking you won't because you don't. Smoke, I mean. So association, it turns out, is as hard to break as habit. Which means it isn't.

Hands

I regularly hear smokers say they can't stop because if they did they wouldn't know what to do with their hands. If we submit this idea to a sanity test I think you will find it fails, miserably.

Tobacco kills three hundred Britons every day, and you want to tell me you do it for something to do with your hands, that you're in the habit of having a cigarette between your fingers and you can't stop because what else would you do? I don't think so. Let me explain where this idea goes wrong.

Which part of your body do you smoke with? Your mouth? No, that's just where you stick the cigarette, but your mouth doesn't really do any work. OK, I'll tell you the answer, it's your hands. Yes, the instant you think of a cigarette your hands go into action. They find the pack, they find the lighter and the ashtray and they open the pack and take one out and light it and then, and only then, is your mouth asked to do any work, which amounts to no more than sucking.

So when you want to smoke it is your hands that receive a signal to go into action, and it is your hands that get the fidgets when you are trying not to smoke, but not because your hands like holding cigarettes, obviously.

After all, what's to stop you doing all that stuff and not actually lighting it? You could even suck on it quite harmlessly, as long as you didn't light it, and that tells you what's missing. The nice feeling of hot smoke in your mouth? No, think again. That's right, nicotine. Your hands feed you with nicotine. That's why, when you are craving a cigarette, your hands want to do something.

You could hold a cigarette, you could suck it, or if that scares you you can hold just about anything, but never again think you can't stop smoking because you need something in your hands.

Fascinating Fact Number 7

Some women stop smoking when they get pregnant, but many don't. Those who continue pass the nicotine they absorb with each cigarette to the foetus, which means the foetus is addicted, and dependent on the mother for each fix.

If the mother stops smoking during pregnancy, the foetus will go through withdrawal from nicotine. Does this mean it is better to carry on smoking? No. Because as far as I know medical staff are not trained to recognise nicotine withdrawal in a newborn baby, let alone treat it.

No-one, to our knowledge, has ever researched how much neo-natal distress has been caused by nicotine withdrawal.

It is therefore better to stop during pregnancy, where the foetus is getting well looked after. Of course, it is better still to stop before pregnancy and avoid the problem altogether.

Use this space to make any comments or note any reminders for yourself.

Tutorial Eight

How nicotine makes you think you like smoking

In this tutorial I am going to be asking five questions:

- Is the perceived pleasure of smoking stopping you stopping?
- If you enjoy smoking, is it also true that you enjoy being a smoker?
- Who enjoys life more, smokers or non-smokers?
- Is smoking as enjoyable as you think it is?
- If it is, is it worth dying for?

The answer to all five questions is going to make it harder for you to justify smoking. You could guess that, couldn't you? What would be the point of this kind of Handbook otherwise? The sad thing is that I'm right. Sorry, but if you read this tutorial you are never again going to be able to say you won't stop smoking because you enjoy it too much, not with a clear conscience, anyway. That excuse is going to be lost to you for ever. You could skip this tutorial, but come on, are you really such a coward?

Is the perceived pleasure of smoking stopping you stopping?

I've talked about the fear of stopping, and this is another part of that, isn't it? The fear that you will never again be able to enjoy a cigarette. It's part of what we call the fear of success.

There are lots of times when you feel you enjoy a smoke. As a reward, after work, when you're relaxing, with friends, with a drink. If the thought of missing all that didn't put you off stopping it would be very surprising. It's enough to make people say they don't want to stop and it's also enough to sabotage an attempt when you do try to stop.

In fact it is possibly the main factor when people say they don't want to stop smoking. I regularly speak to smokers who say they know they should stop but it's their only pleasure. Well, we'll be looking shortly at the sanity of this statement but the fact remains that the majority of smokers, especially younger ones, believe they enjoy it, and they also believe that enjoyment is worth whatever smoking might do to them. They are doing a risk/benefit assessment without knowing they are doing it, in which they assume there is no risk because they're young and there is lots of benefit so actually it's a very quick assessment.

In other words, it doesn't matter how old you are and it doesn't matter how well or otherwise you understand the damage caused by smoking, the fact is you believe there is a benefit.

You must do. Otherwise why would you do it?

Case Study

Brian phoned us to ask about our programmes and, as we always do, we went through his previous attempts to stop and what he thought his issues were. It's a standard we set years ago, that you never offer help to a smoker until you know what help they need.

We could tell straight away that he wasn't ready to do this, that he was phoning because he was under pressure, perhaps from his wife, to do something. And then he said it, those magic words, I enjoy smoking. We know that as long as a smoker believes that they are not going to stop. The secret is not in them stopping enjoying it, but in them stopping BELIEVING they enjoy it. Rather than enrolling him in a programme we simply suggested he join our epsilon research project. He particularly liked the idea of not having to attend an appointment at a clinic.

Brian went out drinking two or three times a week with his friends (this was in the days when you could smoke in pubs) and in the first consultation it became clear that to him the whole social/drinking/smoking thing was an unbreakable triangle. How could we persuade him that the smoking part had nothing to do with the other two parts?

We gave him the logical arguments, all the things you have been reading about here, and someone who wants to believe them is going to do just that, but he didn't want to. On the intellectual level he understood, but on the emotional level he rejected the idea that he didn't enjoy smoking, and this was nothing to do with smoking, it was because to him smoking was the ingredient that kept his circle of friends glued together.

In the end it wasn't the arguments than won him round. It wasn't really, I have to confess, anything we said or did, although I like to think that had some impact at least. Brian was made redundant. That wasn't a complete disaster, because it pushed him to do the thing he had always wanted to do, a diving course. The course cost a lot of money, which he paid for with his redundancy payment, but more importantly you can't smoke if you are a diver, and he wanted to be a diver more than he wanted to smoke. He simply weighed up the relative values of the options available and came to his own conclusion. And his friends in the pub? Did they break up because Brian stopped smoking? Of course they didn't.

Is it true that you enjoy being a smoker?

I don't mean do you enjoy smoking, I mean do you like the fact that you are a smoker? Are you happy that you smoke?I guess the answer to that has to be no, doesn't it, because otherwise why are you reading this Handbook? So we seem to have a conflict. You say you enjoy smoking (of course you might not be saying that, I don't know you, I'm speaking generally), but you aren't happy to be smoking. That doesn't sound right, does it? It's one of the many contradictions in smoking, which I expect you have realised.

How can anyone like doing something but be unhappy

that they do it at the same time? Normally I would say that's unlikely. I mean, for example, either you like playing cricket or you don't. I don't know anyone who plays cricket and says I like doing this but I wish I didn't do it. That kind of conflict is, I imagine, fairly uncommon among cricketers. Similarly I don't know anyone who eats smoked salmon and regrets it. They enjoy smoked salmon and they are pretty well content to be someone who eats it. No conflict there.

Of the tens of thousand of smokers we have dealt with over the years, we know exactly the number who are happy to be smokers, even if they claim to enjoy smoking. It's nil. What can we learn from that conflict? It can only be that being unhappy that you are a smoker is real, and believing you enjoy a cigarette is because you are addicted to nicotine.

Who enjoys life more, smokers or non-smokers?

Smokers are the people who know how to have fun. It's a commonly-held belief, but it is, I'm afraid, tosh. Watch a group of smokers standing outside a bar having a laugh and it would be easy to think it's real, but there are two problems here:

- The non-smokers inside are also having fun, and what's more they're not standing in the rain.

- What the smokers are laughing about is quite likely themselves.

There is undoubtedly a camaraderie among smokers, but is it because there is something inherently more fun-loving about a smoker, or because they stick together as a way to justify what they are doing? Try as I might I can't think why people who smoke should have a better sense of humour than people who don't. You might say they are the people who know how to buck the trend, they are cool, they are rebels, but I'm sorry, I don't associate any of those epithets with drug-taking.

Given that almost every adult smoker in the world wants to be a non-smoker (please, don't let's have that argument again) but there is no such thing as a non-smoker who is miserable because he can't start smoking, on balance non-smokers must be happier than smokers. Don't you think?

Is smoking as enjoyable as you think it is?

This is a pretty crucial question, isn't it? If you have convinced yourself that any risk involved in smoking is outweighed by the benefit, by which you mean enjoyment, and you discover that there isn't any enjoyment, that is going to drive a coach and horses through your justification for smoking.

Aha, but you know there is enjoyment. OK, maybe not all the time, but you know there are some cigarettes you really enjoy, and they would be hard to give up.

Some cigarettes? Just a minute. Surely if a cigarette is nice, well, aren't two cigarettes twice as nice? If a cigarette is a pleasure, then every cigarette must be a pleasure. If it's a pleasure one minute, how can it possibly not be a pleasure the next? Come on now, either it's good or it isn't. So why do people enjoy smoking some times more than others? It's a good question. No, it's a vital question. And it will not surprise you that I am going to answer it, in some detail.

Which cigarettes do you enjoy the most? No, don't tell me, let me guess. First thing in the morning? After a meal? After work? When you get out of the cinema? I could go on. Have you noticed, though, that these situations all have something in common? They are all after a period of abstinence. In other words, the longer it is since you smoked, the more enjoyable it is to smoke. It's not unreasonable, when you think about it. When is it most enjoyable to eat? When you're hungry. When is it most enjoyable to drink? When you're thirsty. When is it most enjoyable to rest? When you're tired.

So why is it most enjoyable to smoke when you haven't smoked for a while? No, come on, I want you to think about this as if your life depended on it, which come to think about it it might. Yes, as you have already learned, the nicotine in your body is quickly lost and it puts you into subliminal nicotine deprivation. The lower the level of nicotine, the more you are going to enjoy getting a nicotine top-up.

Let's just go back to one particular cigarette, the first one in the morning. To most smokers, this is the most important smoke of the day, and often involves one cigarette after another. Perhaps you can't imagine not needing to smoke first thing, and that scares you. So what is it about that first cigarette? Yes, it's the longest you go without smoking.

It's really rather simple. You are in deeper withdrawal at that time than at any other. (In fact, it would be reasonable to say that at that moment you have stopped smoking.) Alright, that doesn't sound so surprising, but think now about what exactly that means.

It means, and here there should be a roll of drums, that the pleasure of smoking isn't actually pleasure at all. It's the relief of displeasure. Here's a chart:

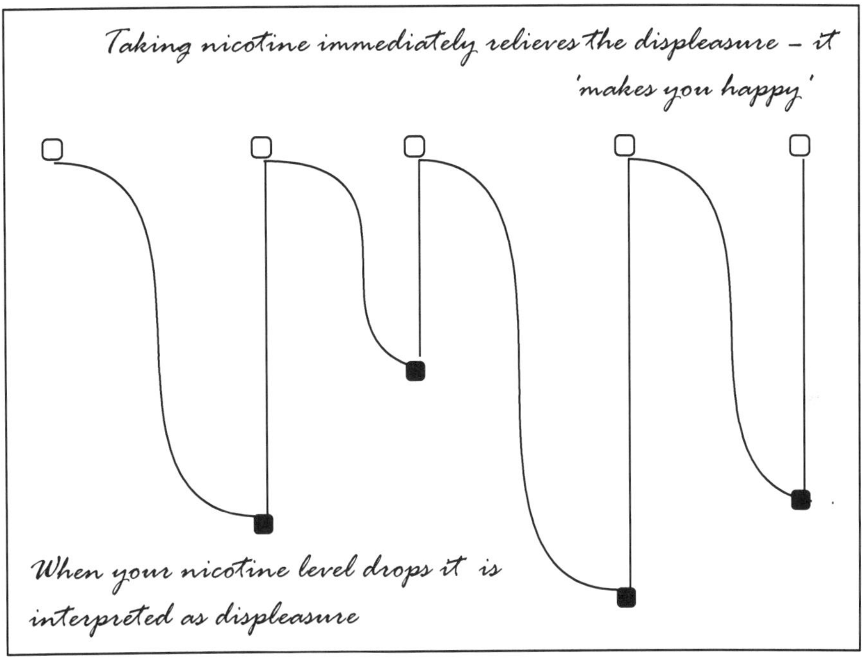

Every time you put a cigarette out your nicotine level drops, until it reaches the trigger that makes you smoke. That trigger, like hunger and thirst, is registered as unpleasant. Inevitably, therefore, when you get a fix and the withdrawal goes away, your poor old brain interprets this as pleasure. Of course, it is nothing of the kind. If you didn't have the displeasure, you wouldn't need the pleasure.

Hold on, though, surely I'm not saying there is no such thing as a pleasant smoke? That's going too far, isn't it? Well, it depends on what you mean by pleasure. If you with a glass of wine in your hand and good friends around you, you are already in a state of pleasure. If they all light up and so do you, and it's been an hour or two since you smoked so you are in subliminal nicotine deprivation, it's not hard to guess that the cigarette is going to be good.

If, on the other hand, you have a cold and your wife has just sent you outside the back door in February because you want to smoke, I strongly suspect that, even with the same level of nicotine deprivation, that cigarette is not going to be a huge pleasure. In other words. much of the pleasure of smoking is situation-dependent. If you are already enjoying yourself, it is easier to enjoy a cigarette. Is it any different from the contrast between a cream cake with a perfect cup of coffee in a cosy tea-room in front of a log fire, or that same cream cake in a tent with the rain dripping down your neck when you take the children camping?

If you habitually smoke in enjoyable situations, which you do, you are bound to have developed a belief that smoking is part of that enjoyment. Sadly, it isn't. Even in that situation, it is still nothing more than drug-taking. We know this because people who don't smoke enjoy those situations just as much. Unfortunately, over the years you have had this false information fed to your brain so many times it seems hard to let go of it. But let go of it you must. It's a lie, and it's a dangerous one, and here I'm afraid, it's my duty to remind you, smoking kills.

And now I am going to play my trump card. I want you to think back, however many years it is, to when you first smoked. It was more than forty years ago for me, and I can remember it in detail. What I want to know is this: did you enjoy your first cigarette? Not the second one, the first one. If you think you did, this next bit doesn't work, not because I'm wrong but because there was an extenuating fact, most likely that someone in your household smoked and you were already addicted by passive smoking, so it proves nothing.

But that aside, let's assume you remember it as unpleasant. It tasted bad, perhaps it made you nauseous, a bit light headed. You persisted, I know, but I think you would be the first to admit it wasn't because you loved it so much you just had to do it again, it was because of social pressure to conform. Your friends didn't react like that, so subconsciously perhaps you knew you had to learn to smoke. Now I've use the word react, haven't I? Think about this: why did you react to the first cigarette like that?

If you've said you don't know, tut tut. If you've said because tobacco smoke is poisonous, go to the front of the class. Tobacco smoke is the most poisonous substance you will ever have to deal with. So, you tell me, if tobacco smoke is poisonous, how do you think you are likely to react to it? That's right, you will have a poison reaction, which means it will at the very least taste bad, and probably make you nauseous and dizzy, funnily enough exactly what happened perhaps. Tobacco smoke is poisonous so it tastes bad and is unpleasant to inhale. This is incontrovertible.

Hold on, though, you enjoy smoking. This looks like trouble. How can it be? Well, let me tell you. You adapted to the poisons. This was explained in Tutorial 5, so please don't say you didn't know. That adaptation does a very interesting thing.

It stops your body telling you you are taking a poison,

and then it makes you demand the poison. What it doesn't do is stop tobacco being poisonous. In other words, it creates the belief that the poisons are pleasant.

That's nasty.

Is it worth dying for?

Alright, you force me to do this. So you really do enjoy smoking, and yes, you are right and I am wrong. I know, unlikely, but let's think the unthinkable for a moment.

That leaves one very big question. No matter how good smoking is, is it worth dying for? No, I take that back, let's not talk about dying, let's talk about emphysema, struggling to breathe every waking minute, waiting to die. Or having a cancerous lung removed. or a leg, or let's make that two legs.

One thing we never do in our work is lecture people about the evils of smoking, and I promised way back at the start that I wasn't going to do that. But even if I keep my promise I am obliged to admit the facts, aren't I? Smoking does all these things. It's not necessarily doing them to you, right now, but it undeniably does them.

But that's only part of the picture. Let's turn this on its head and imagine you had never smoked. There you are, weighing up the pros and cons of starting to smoke. On the plus side:

- Smokers says they enjoy it and it helps them to relieve stress and boredom and make friends.

And on the minus side:

- It will typically cost £2000 a year of taxed income, it will turn you into a social leper and it will destroy your lungs.

So there you are, weighing this up, and you think, yep, cheap at half the price, let's go for it. Can you imagine anyone actually doing that? Can you imagine anyone who smokes, knowing all of this, encouraging a young person to start smoking? Can you imagine anyone saying they would rather smoke than take the family on a super holiday every year, or buy a new car? And mean it?

No, no-one would say these things. But what they do is carry on smoking, because they enjoy it. You know what the problem is, don't you?

They're not thinking. And why aren't they thinking? Because, and I just know you have heard this before, the addiction to nicotine turns your brain to mush. Saying you can't stop or won't stop because you enjoy it too much is rubbish. It's not you talking, because you're not that daft. It's the drug talking.

So what can you do about this? It's simple really. You have a choice. You can smoke for the rest of your life on a false premise and listen to the sound of laughter as the tobacco companies and the government romp to the bank with your money, or you can refuse to be abused.

Fascinating Fact Number 8

If there are about 14 million smokers in the UK, and if on

average they smoke about fifteen cigarettes a day. That's 210 million cigarettes burned each day, or 76,650,000,000 a year. No-one has ever calculated the environmental cost of that much smoke going into the atmosphere, or even whether there is one.

And that's only the UK.

Use this space to make any comments or
note any reminders for yourself.

Tutorial Nine

How smoking makes you believe it relaxes you

Here's a typical scene from a three-part British television crime drama:

In the first episode, the police keep finding bodies and getting frustrated that they can't solve the crimes. In the second episode they arrest a man and go to the pub because it's all over, even though you know it's not because this is only part two so there must be more. Then, in the third episode, they find a particularly gruesome murder. Cut to the back of the police station. The Inspector is on the fire escape, smoking. The Sergeant comes out to have one himself.

'Oh, hello Guv'nor. Smoking eh? I thought you'd packed it up.'

'Yes Bill, but after that last body, well, ...'

Yes, the Sergeant knows what he means. It's enough to make anyone start smoking again. He and the Inspector commiserate with each other and enjoy a nice relaxing smoke. The poor dears. They've been through a lot.

Alright, so what exactly is going on here? What is the scriptwriter telling us? That they are especially stressed. Stressed enough to start smoking again. Smoking is writers' shorthand for stress. It's not until you see a policeman, or a single mother whose child is missing, or even a doctor who has just lost a patient, that you appreciate the terrible stress they are under. And when you see them smoking, you know immediately.

It is not only lazy writing, it's nonsense. Yes, people smoke when they are stressed, and yes, ex-smokers go back to smoking when they are stressed, but why do they do that? Do they do it because it relaxes them, or because they THINK it's going to relax them? Do they do it because they saw someone on television doing it? Actually, that's not as crass as it sounds because it's true, TV has enormous influence, and it has the power, in one such scene, to influence millions of people, to confirm what they always suspected, that when you are stressed it's a good idea to smoke. It doesn't matter that it's not true. An idea doesn't have to be true for people to believe it. Ask any politician.

Oh no, I hear you say, smoking definitely helps me when I'm stressed. Well, look, I know you feel better when you smoke, I admit it, but now I am going to tell you why it's a trick.

Turn back to the chart in the previous tutorial, the one with the up and down lines that show displeasure from not smoking and pleasure when you smoke, the one that shows that the pleasure isn't actually pleasure, it's the relief of displeasure. This same chart applies equally to stress.

Stressors are events that your body reacts to in a certain way. If you ever get a stress headache you know what I'm talking about. One kind of stressor is the one I was talking about a lot earlier. If you burn your hand you react by removing it from the source of heat. The heat is a stressor.

Some stress reactions are automatic, like this one, and some are learned, like having a strong drink after a hard day at work. If you are wearing a new pair of shoes and they hurt your feet, the shoes are a stressor and you relieve stress by taking them off. This is both automatic and learned, because an animal with a less developed brain would take time to realise that taking the shoes off relieved the pain. On the other hand an animal with a less developed brain would buy the right-sized shoes, even if they weren't so fashionable, so forget that one.

Do people learn to smoke as a direct consequence of stress? The answer to that is a resounding no. If smoking relieved stress, a lot more people would do it. Remember, eighty percent of the population of most Western countries don't smoke, so if smoking is so great at relieving stress they don't seem to have heard about it. So what we don't have is a great way to relieve stress that people learn about and use. What we do have is a lot of people who smoke and claim it relieves stress, and that would seem to me to be a conflict of ideas.

Back to the chart. When you are addicted to nicotine, every time you put a cigarette out the nicotine level drops and produces displeasure. But what it also does is increase stress. This is hardly surprising, because after all displeasure is a stressor. Therefore, every time you put a cigarette out you go into subliminal nicotine deprivation, and that is a stressor, and your brain knows the way to relieve the problem is to light a cigarette. So what you have done is develop a cycle of stress and stress relief by smoking. The sad fact is, though, that smoking doesn't relieve any other stress except the stress of not having smoked for a while. Smoking creates stress and then relieves that stress, but it's a stress that you wouldn't have and therefore wouldn't need to relieve if you didn't smoke. Smoking makes you believe it relieves stress when all it does is create stress and relieve the same stress. It is completely self-defeating.

Taking shoes off that are too tight relieves one stress only - the pain in your feet. Removing your hand from the source of heat relieves one stress only - the pain in your hand. Smoking a cigarette relieves one stress only - the withdrawal from nicotine.

And just as taking your shoes off does not in any other way make your life less stressful, smoking a cigarette doesn't make your life less stressful.

But that's where the analogy falls apart. You might take your shoes off once a day. All the things you do to relieve a specific stressor are done only from time to time. But how many cigarettes do you smoke? 20 a day? Let's go with that number anyway. That means that twenty times every day you go into withdrawal from nicotine and raise your stress level, and twenty times every day you relieve that stress by smoking. Is it any wonder that you believe the thing you do more than anything else to relieve stress is the thing that relieves stress?

As a stress reliever tobacco is pretty useless. OK, it's true that it's a psychotropic drug, which means it does have some power to alter your brain chemistry, but it's a very weak one. Alcohol is much better.

Is nicotine a sedative or a stressor?

Talking of alcohol, it is known that drinking can have two quite opposite effects. One drink relaxes you, perhaps two do, but the more you drink the more stressed you become (i.e. aggressive, until you're unconscious, anyway).

Tobacco also has two quite different effects, depending on how you use it. Have you ever noticed that when you've got some job to do that requires concentration, filling in a complicated form for example, that you will light a cigarette and take the odd puff while it burns away in the ashtray? But when you are stressed you don't do that. You take deep drags on it as if your life depended on it. In the first example, nicotine is stimulating your brain, but in the second it is suppressing your brain.

How does it do this? Well, again, there hasn't been enough research, but in the Institute we do our research by means of observation, and what we have observed is this: first, nicotine is a brain stimulant in small doses and a brain suppressor in large doses. That is simply the paradoxical way all drugs work.

But then there is another effect. When you light a cigarette you are in subliminal nicotine deprivation, remember, so you are finding it a little harder to concentrate because the withdrawal symptoms are preventing your brain working properly (because they want it to concentrate on getting a cigarette). What happens when you take short puffs as you do your work is that the nicotine prevents withdrawal symptoms and allows your brain to function properly.

On the other hand, if you draw on the cigarette heavily, what happens is that it puts a lot of carbon monoxide into your brain. While you smoke a cigarette about 10% of your brain's oxygen is replaced by CO. Carbon monoxide has an immediate effect on the brain - it suppresses it. The brain needs a good supply of oxygen to function properly. On 90% oxygen it can't do that. So smoking heavily suppresses brain activity, which has the effect of making you feel calmer.

Of course there is another way to use carbon monoxide. Connect up the exhaust of your car to the inside and turn the engine on. You will gradually lose consciousness as the CO pushes out all the oxygen.

What you do every time you light a cigarette, even if you think it is relaxing you, is in fact practising suicide.

Smoking and breathing

When you smoke for stress, you inhale deeply. Thus you learn to breathe deeply when you're stressed, which is a good thing. The problem (apart from smoking not being a good thing) is that now you can't cope with stress without breathing deeply and you think the only way you can do that is to smoke.

There are two ways to get out of this dead-end. Use herbal cigarettes, in the short term, to inhale deeply on something that is not addictive, and/or learn the breathing exercise in Project 6 and use it regularly.

If nicotine did relieve stress, would it be a good way to do it?

The answer to this is obviously no, simply because the price you would pay for that relaxation would be too high. The only reason you even consider it acceptable is because it's your drug of choice - you already use it and because, remember, nicotine turns your brain to mush, you are incapable of making a rational judgment about it.

Throwing yourself under a bus will stop you ever being stressed again, but it's a bit drastic, isn't it? Well, smoking is like throwing yourself under a bus in slow motion. I can think of any number of things you could do to be less stressed, without smoking. The list is so long I'm not even going to mention it, which would be silly. Look, imagine this scene:

A woman from another planet goes to see her GP.

'Doctor, I'm so stressed, you've got to give me something.'

'Alright, take these.'

'What are they?'

'They're called cigarettes.'

'I see. How do I take them?'

'You put this end in your mouth and you light the other

end. Smoke comes out of it and you inhale this.'

The woman looks doubtful.

'And will this make me less stressed?'

'Uhuh, it's all the rage on Earth.'

'Oh, right. I suppose there aren't any side effects?'

'No, well yes, some.'

'Really, you mean someone has been made unwell by it?'

'Um, yes.'

'I see, well you must know what you're doing. By the way, have many people been made unwell by it? And how unwell are you talking about?'

'Alright, look, a few thousand Earthlings die each day.'

Point made?

I'm going to be talking a lot, later, about staying stopped, but the belief in the stress-relieving property of smoking is the single major reason why people start smoking again, often years after they have stopped.

Rationally, they know it's not true, that it isn't going to help. but I've already said, once a smoker always someone who used to be a smoker. When you start smoking you give away the ability to think rationally about smoking. Ten years after you have stopped, twenty years even, you might come under some terrible stress and someone offers you a cigarette and instead of responding rationally to the idea you just take it. There is almost no way you can stop this happening.

Am I being pessimistic? No, I'm being realistic. The belief in the stress-relieving property of tobacco goes so deep that you will probably never escape it. In fact it is the reason so many people start smoking again not within years but within months.

Does that mean you are doomed to go back to smoking at some time once you have stopped? Yes and no. Wouldn't you just know there isn't a simple answer? Anyway, this tutorial isn't about staying stopped, so lots more about that later. For now I want to make the point as forcefully as I can.

Smoking doesn't relieve stress.

And another thought

Are you worried about your smoking? My guess is that you are, on the basis that you're reading this Handbook. Been worried about it for long? Tried to stop and failed? Uhuh, I see. Would you say that all of this has made you stressed about smoking? Uhuh, I see. Would you like to stop being stressed about smoking?

So stop.

Fascinating Fact Number 9

There is a paradoxical effect of new drugs for smokers to

stop. Every time one is introduced by the NHS, hoards of people go on it. Some people succeed with it, of course, but naturally the great majority don't, as in the nature of all drugs.

There is then a period, after all the hullabaloo has died down, when people simply don't want to stop smoking. Failure to stop, especially with a drug product that has been hailed as the best thing ever, destroys the motivation of a lot of smokers for a long time.

Use this space to make any comments or note any reminders for yourself.

Tutorial Ten

What you need to know about smoking & eating

You're probably thinking this tutorial is going to tell you how not to put weight on when you stop smoking.

Well, yes, of course I'm going to be talking about that, but believe me there's a lot more to this subject than weight gain. Smoking and eating are closely connected, in more ways than you think, so even if you're not worried about your weight don't skip this tutorial, will you?

Alright, first things first, why do people put on weight when they stop smoking? For the same reason they put on weight when they do anything else - because they are eating too much. It's not complicated; the more you eat the heavier you get, and the less you burn the heavier you get. If you put eighty litres of petrol in your car it gets heavier. I don't know what eighty litres of petrol weighs but I expect it's not something you would want to carry around all day. As you burn that petrol the car gets lighter. You need the petrol in order to run the car, but there is a weight-to-power formula for every car.

Likewise for every person. You eat and get heavier. If you don't burn that food you stay heavier. The difference between a car and a person is that you can't keep stuffing a car.

So, why do people eat too much when they are stopping smoking? I wish I had a pound for every smoker who has told me it was because they needed something to do with their hands. Really, what silliness this is. Something to do with their hands? I can think of, let's say, five thousand things they could do with their hands that don't involve stuffing their faces.

Putting weight on has absolutely nothing to do with your hands, it's got to do with your mouth. In which case, the question remains, why do people eat more when they stop smoking?

Sugar. It works like this. When you smoke, your body immediately recognises that you are poisoning yourself and it produces a toxic reaction, a large part of which is increased activity in your adrenal glands. Smoking a cigarette, in other words, produces the same stress reaction as meeting a gang of drunks in the street on a dark night. This is because your body chemistry doesn't differentiate between stressors. If it's scared it's scared, and 4865 poisons down your throat is easily enough to scare it. It doesn't matter how many years you have smoked for, your body never gets used to it, and it never stops producing a stress reaction.

One of the main effects of the production of adrenaline is an increased blood-sugar level. This is because if you are going to have to fight or flee your muscles need more sugar. It is this effect that curbs your appetite when you smoke instead of eating. High blood sugar fools the body into thinking it doesn't need food. Young women do this to stay thin, and it's pretty dangerous.

If you smoke twenty times a day, your body gets twenty sugar rushes each day. Then you decide to stop smoking. You're craving nicotine, but your body also remembers that just as nicotine relieves the need for sugar, sugar relieves the need for nicotine. They are, to some extent, interchangeable. So you eat a biscuit, your blood sugar goes up and that makes you feel a little better. You don't need a cigarette for a little while. An interesting thing happens, though, if your blood sugar goes up. You produce insulin to balance it out. If you eat sugar sensibly, you produce insulin sensibly, but if you eat a biscuit, which is almost all refined carbohydrate, that one biscuit can trigger a slight overproduction of insulin, depending on how your pancreas is working. This pushes your blood sugar slightly below the optimum level, and that tells your body to look for more sugar.

This doesn't happen to everyone, but it certainly happens to some. And if it does, then you end up eating more and more. It doesn't, by the way, have to be sweet food. Fats and sugars work together in a way I'm not going to explain here but overeating, any kind of food, at this time is likely to be for this reason.

So much for the science. Of course there are other reasons why some people eat when they stop smoking. For some, it's a comfort thing, and for others it's a self-fulfilling prophecy - everyone says you eat more so you do, almost as if you're following their advice. And of course there are other psychological triggers like boredom and so on.

What is so interesting is that in our main programme for

smokers, Phoenix, in which we stop the withdrawal symptoms and therefore the craving for nicotine, it is almost unheard of for patients to crave food, and this would seem to demonstrate that the sugar connection is the main issue.

If this happens to you, what should you do about it? The answer is in the old joke, you know, the one about the fantastic new diet in which you can eat absolutely anything you like, you're just not allowed to swallow. It's not exactly that, but I couldn't think of anywhere else in this tutorial to put a joke. There is a good way and a bad way to eat when you stop smoking. First, a bad way. This is a typical conversation one of our nurses might have with a patient:

'So tell me about your diet.'

'Oh, I eat very healthily.'

'Good, tell me a bit more, though. For example, what did you have for breakfast this morning.'

'Cereal.'

'I see. Is that it?'

'And coffee with milk, low-fat, and one sugar, and two cigarettes.'

'Right, and tell me about a typical lunch.'

'Oh I always eat lunch.'

'Like what?'

'I have sandwiches usually.'

'Uhuh, and what do you have in your sandwiches?'

'Oh it varies. Cold meat, cheese, you know.'

'Anything else, I mean in the sandwich?'

'No.'

'What kind of bread?'

'White.'

'Right, now let's look at dinner. Do you cook in the evening?'

'Usually. Pasta, some fish, all sorts. And I eat plenty of fruit.'

'Alright. Now, what do you drink?'

'Well, two or three cups of tea in the day, a couple of coffees. Cola at lunchtime.'

'How much cola?'

'Oh, one of those small bottles, but it's diet cola, so that's alright, isn't it?'

No, but we'll come back to that. We see worse diets than this, much worse. We see people whose daily diet is putting them at risk of death, and I promise I am not exaggerating. The most common risk we see, though, is of diabetes. So here's what's wrong with this patient's diet, even before she stops smoking:

Almost all breakfast cereals are heavily laced with sugar. Ready-made muesli is especially bad. This much sugar first thing is bad news. Breakfast should always include protein. It doesn't have to be a lot; a boiled egg, some peanut butter on toast, some real muesli with nuts and seeds as well as fruit will do.

Coffee and a cigarette will do nothing but compound the damage done by the sugar in the cereal. And full-fat milk, please, and if you don't know why look it up somewhere. (The last time I was in New York I sat in a café and watched office workers breakfasting on coffee and a Danish. This is diabetes waiting to happen.)

White bread has no nutritional value and just pushes the sugar level up. When you're eating a sandwich all white bread does is stop you getting mustard on your fingers. And one important word here - salad. I don't want to see you eating any sandwich without lashings of green stuff in it. Why? Because a sandwich should be a balanced meal, and a meal without green stuff is not balanced.

Dinner. Pasta is alright, but what is white pasta? That's right, refined carbohydrate, which is another word for sugar. It may not taste like sugar when you eat it but believe me it becomes sugar not long afterwards. Try wholemeal pasta, it's much tastier. Or even mix half and half. And a pasta meal should have veggies with it, please, and/or fruit afterwards.

A word about fruit. Sugar. What is fruit? It's water and sugar. It's good, because there are also lots of vitamins, but don't do what some of our patients do, which is to imagine they have a great diet because they are eating fruit all day. I met a woman once who was on some diet that meant eating sixteen apples every day. That's just plain barmy.

Now to drinks. There's nothing wrong with tea and coffee, in moderation. We see patients who are on twenty cups a day, and that is not what we mean by moderation. (Interestingly, they almost always cut right down when they stop smoking.) And cola drinks are in general bad news. Don't get me wrong, I drink the stuff, but once or twice a year, on a really hot summer's day, ice cold. We see patients on two litres of the stuff every day (although they stop that too when they stop smoking).

A word about diet drinks. Aspartame. I won't say anything about it, because I could get sued by the manufacturers, but I have never let my children consume it, so say no more. One of the biggest favours you can do for your body, after

stopping smoking of course, is to cut down on the sugar. You might have noticed I haven't talked about fats. I don't care about fats. I don't care about cholesterol. I care about sugar. Consult any reputable author on nutrition and you will know why.

When you stop smoking the most important dietary advice is to keep your sugar intake low, your protein intake high, and drink plenty of fluids. A word about fluids. Water. Yes folks, it's God's gift to mankind. If you are bad at water I can sympathise, because I used to be. I just didn't get thirsty. Then I started having pains in my kidneys and I suddenly found myself doing something about it. What can you do to drink more water? Well there's water and then there's water. I don't care if it comes from the tap or the supermarket, but cold water, straight from the fridge, is more palatable than at room temperature. If you like fizzy drinks, buy fizzy water. Put some fruit juice in it, say half and half. Then there are herb teas. There are lots of ways you can get your fluid intake up if you really think about it. Water is good for so many reasons, but when you stop smoking it is going to help to detoxify you. Detox symptoms can mimic withdrawal symptoms, and not a few people start smoking again for the wrong reason - because they think they are craving nicotine when actually they are eliminating nicotine nicely.

And now we come to the subject you have been patiently waiting for me to tell you about, tomatoes. What is the connection between tomatoes and smoking, and why does it matter?

The tobacco plant is a member of the Nightshade family or, if you are a Latin scholar, Solenaceae. Plant families all, as you might imagine, have common characteristics, as do human families. Your body is able to make a connection between plants of the same family; it recognises a family resemblance. And another member of the Nightshade family is the tomato.

Now I know that a tomato does not look or taste like a cigarette, but I'm talking here on the molecular level. When you eat a tomato, your body reads its entire molecular structure, and when it does that it makes a match with some molecules it already knows - tobacco molecules. And guess what? If you are at that moment in withdrawal from nicotine and your body sees tomato molecules, yes, it will try to use those molecules to satisfy the craving for nicotine. In other words, a tomato can be used as a nicotine substitute.

So is this a good thing or a bad thing? I mean, surely you

could then eat tomatoes to help you stop needing tobacco? Sadly, no. You see, if you trigger the receptors for nicotine, whether you do it with nicotine or a nicotine substitute (tomato) what you do is to maintain those receptors in an active state. If they see nicotine, they are satisfied, but when that nicotine, or tomato, runs out, they need to be replenished. So, far from satisfying you when you stop smoking, tomatoes have the opposite effect, they keep you addicted. I'm sorry I've only got what sounds like bad news on this, but you need to know these things.

Not everyone is affected by this. In fact very few are, but if you are you need to take this seriously. How do you know if you are? The simple way is to look at your diet. Do you eat tomatoes very regularly? And by tomatoes I include anything and everything made from them, so that means ketchup, sauces, pizza, pasta, do I really need to spell it out? Oh, and baked beans. Think about this - if you put one baked bean on your tongue, what will you taste? Not bean, but tomato. At that point your body has seen tomato and will use it to keep you addicted. So when I say no tomato, funnily enough that's exactly what I mean.

So paradoxically, the less you like tomatoes, and tomato-flavoured food, the less all of this matters. How serious is this? Well, I'll give you a real example.

Case Study

Madeleine joined The Phoenix Programme and we told her, as we tell all patients, not to eat tomatoes. She was a nurse and she understood the science. The next day, though, she rang to say the treatment had stopped working - she was craving nicotine. We asked all sorts of questions and then we came to tomatoes. Oh no, she said, I've been very careful about that. Sure? Well, she said, I had lunch at my mother's house yesterday. I told her about this but I'll just ring to check. Her mother fished an empty condiment jar out from the recycling and read the ingredients. Tomato. It comprised less than one percent of the meal, but tomato is tomato. Madeleine carried on with the treatment and within 24 hours it kicked back in again. And interestingly she then remembered that in both of her pregnancies she stopped smoking but had had a craving for tomatoes. She even did a survey of her nursing colleagues and discovered that those who smoked ate more tomatoes than those who didn't. Interesting or what?

Have you read this stuff in any other book about stopping smoking? No. Well, remember my promises at the beginning of the Handbook? I said I would be telling you things you don't know, didn't I? Do I keep my promises? I should think so.

The other members of the Nightshade family you are likely to eat, assuming you don't put Deadly Nightshade leaves in your salads, are potato, capsicum (that's peppers to you and me) and aubergine (which my American friends call eggplant). Don't worry too much about these though, because for reasons we don't know they don't seem to cause the same problem. Unless, that is, you have a craving for any of them, in which case they might. Actually, we had a West Indian patient who had the same reaction with chilli pepper, which she put in all her cooking. As soon as she stopped using it, she stopped craving a cigarette.

We occasionally get a call from a smoker who says they

stopped a while ago but have never stopped craving and it's driving them nuts. The first thing we check is passive smoking, but if they're not doing that we ask about tomatoes. They listen with surprise, but then they go off and stop eating them and they ring back a week later and say thank you, I wish I had known that before, the craving has just gone away. We love it.

Oh, I forgot to mention. The not eating tomato thing is only for four days after you stop smoking.

Phew.

Fascinating Fact Number 10

The British government, bless them, say that 80% of smokers want to stop. This figure is not derived from any research we can find. It seems to have rather a lot to do with the Health Department's close relationship with the drug companies. The more people they say want to stop, the more funding the smoking cessation services will get, and the more money will be spent with the drug companies.

If you take only the people who say they actively want to stop smoking, it's under 10%. But then since no-one has ever defined what want means, it's all rather academic anyway.

Use this space to make any comments or
note any reminders for yourself.

Tutorial Eleven

What happens after you stop

There are reckoned to be 4865 biologically-active substances in tobacco smoke. Here are some of them:

Carbon monoxide, nicotine, acetaldehyde, acetone, NOx, formic acid, hydrogen cyanide, catechol, ammonia, benzene, acrolein, acrylonitrile, phenol, formaldehyde, carbazole, 2-nitropropane, N-nitrosonornicotine, 4- (methylnitrosamino)-1-(3-pyridil)-1-butanone, N-nitrosoanabasine, N-nitrosodiethanolomine, N-nitrosopyrrolodine, N-nitrosodimethylamine, N-nitrosomethylethylamine, N-nitrosodiethylamine, N-nitrosodi-n-propylamine, N-nitrosodi-n-butylamine, N-nitrosopiperidine, hydrazine, urethane, vinyl chloride, benzanthracine, benzopyrene, 5-methylcrysene, dibenzacridine, 2-napthylamine, 4-aminobiphenyl, 2-toluidine, polonium-210. And so on, ad nauseam.

Now you know what I mean by poisonous. If you weren't scared before you are now. But it's not why I included this information. It means just about nothing to me, not being a chemist, but for good measure, in case you are, here is a list of the compounds you have been inhaling, under their major groupings, with the number of individual compounds in brackets:

Amines, imides, lactones (240); carboxylic acids, anhydrides (240); esters (475); aldehydes (110); ketones (520); alcohols (380); phenols (285); amines (200); N-nitrosamines (922); N-heterocyclics (920); hydrocarbons (755); nitriles (105); carbohydrates (45); ethers (310).

What's surprising is not that people get ill, but that anyone stays alive. The human body is pretty resilient isn't it? You can do all that to it, every day, maybe twenty times a day, and not die. Of course, the secret is in the quantity. You actually only inhale minute amounts of these substances at any one time.

The long-term effect, though, is that they are accumulated in your body, in your lungs and your arteries mainly. It's why smokers not only get cancer but also why tobacco smoke simply breaks down lung tissue.

The toxins in tobacco smoke are of three kinds, in that they do three kinds of damage. There are:

- Carcinogens - they generate cancers.
- Mutagens - they alter your genes, so you pass on faulty genes to your children.
- Teratogens - they cause malformations in your offspring.

The simple way to think of them, though, is that they come embedded in a thick tar that sticks to everything. In fact you might be interested to know how much tar:

Tar consumed over 20 years of smoking

Cigarettes per day	60	438g	1.75kg	2.63kg	3.5kg	3.94kg	5.26kg
	50	365g	1.46kg	2.19kg	2.92kg	3.29kg	4.38kg
	40	292g	1.17kg	1.75kg	2.34kg	2.63kg	3.5kg
	30	219g	876g	1.31kg	1.75kg	1.97kg	2.63kg
	20	146g	584g	876g	1.17kg	1.31kg	1.75kg
	10	73g	292g	438g	584g	657g	876g
		1	4	6	8	9	12
	Mg tar in each cigarette						

No-one is saying all this tar is in you now, because you don't necessarily smoke the whole cigarette, and some of the tar comes back out as you smoke, and I shouldn't be surprised if no-one has ever done the research to find out what proportion sticks to your lungs.

Alright, we've all seen pictures of lungs clogged up with tar but I'm not sure anyone has ever actually measured it. Still, what's for sure is that right now, if you are an average smoker, you are carrying some extra weight.

Have you ever had a ticklish cough first thing in the morning? Have you ever coughed up tar-coloured phlegm? The reason is that your lungs are self-cleaning. If they are irritated they produce a cough to eliminate the irritant. The coughing is your lungs attempting to get rid of tar. The best way to stop the cough is, perversely, to smoke. When the lungs see more smoke coming they give up trying to clear out the old tar and concentrate on absorbing the new tar.

When you stop smoking your lungs don't know you've stopped smoking. They just think it's the dawn of a bright new day and like every other morning a load of noxious smoke is coming down any minute. When it doesn't they think, oh, maybe we could get rid of some of this tar and they produce a cough. This can be slight or it can be a lot, there's no knowing what to expect.

We had a patient once who complained that the treatment we gave her was staining her teeth, but we had to point out that it couldn't do that, the staining was coming from the tar she was breathing up from her lungs. Still, better out than in.

The staining on some smokers' fingers, by the way, is not nicotine. That's what people tend to call them, isn't it, nicotine-stained fingers, but since nicotine represents only about ten percent of the toxins in a cigarette, it's not a reasonable thing to say. It's tar.

If you've been smoking for many years, when you stop your body is going to try to eliminate toxins. Those toxins are at the moment bedded into your lungs but during detoxification they pass through your body and can cause mischief. There's the cough, but toxins breathed out through the mouth can cause mouth ulcers too. Oozing out through the skin can cause all sorts of skin problems. There can be headaches and stomach aches. Muscle pain is not uncommon. You might well be tired for a few days. Some people are so exhausted they can hardly move. The toxins compromise the immune system and there can be opportunistic infections. Some people become depressed. Some people get constipated, because tobacco stimulates the bowels and they have been using it, unintentionally, as a laxative for years.

On the other hand, a lot of people have none of these symptoms at all. In fact some people get a sudden burst of energy when they stop smoking. Obviously, to a large extent how bad the detox symptoms are is going to depend on you, on how many you smoked, how strong they were, how long you smoked for, but also on your level of fitness, your diet and the amount of exercise you take.

And these are the key to detoxifying. We have known people start smoking again because of the detox symptoms they experienced, which is of course daft, but on the other hand if you don't understand what it is and also you don't know how long it might go on for you might easily be tempted. So we have some standard advice we give to our patients to help with detoxification:

- Fluid intake, preferably water, should be high
- Get plenty of exercise, preferably outdoors
- Take high-dose vitamin C and perhaps B-complex
- Use the breathing exercise explained in Project 5.

Smoking and asthma

"Cigarette smoking has two opposing effects on the bronchi (air tubes) of the lungs. On the one hand the complex mixture of tars and combustion products includes many allergens (substances that allergy-prone individuals are likely to react to), and therefore certain people tend to become allergic to cigarette smoke. Since allergy in the lungs leads to asthma, smoking tends to make allergic smokers worse.

On the other hand the smoke also contains nicotine and other drug-like constituents which relax the bronchi and loosen the mucus so it can be coughed up. Many asthmatics find that a deep draw on a cigarette helps them cough up their phlegm and breathe more easily. Fifty years ago doctors used to recommend smoking to asthmatics for this reason.

Thus smoking is doing two things at once, one good and one bad, for asthmatics. The 'good' reaction - relieving the breathing - is fast and easily noticed. The 'bad' effect - aggravating the allergy - is slow and not easily recognised by the sufferer; it takes many years to cause a gradual and insidious deterioration of lung function.

Asthmatics who stop smoking may find their asthma aggravated. Smokers who never had asthma may even develop it, for the first time in their lives, after stopping. This is because they no longer enjoy the short-term relief afforded by the smoke. We therefore consider it essential that allergy to smoke (where it exists) is treated at the same time as stopping smoking.

In practice this is easily brought about for those patients in The Phoenix Programme, because Addiction Neutralisation Therapy also reduces the allergy. Experience so far shows that patients who are neutralised for tobacco smoke do not develop asthma, and those who are already asthmatic get better, not worse."

(With thanks to Dr DLJ Freed, MD)

Whatever you feel like when you stop, the first thing to do is to assess whether what you are experiencing is withdrawal symptoms or detox symptoms. It's not always easy to tell the difference (except in Phoenix because you won't be having withdrawal symptoms), but one major difference is the time-span. If the symptoms continue for more than four days, and you are definitely not passive smoking or eating tomato, then they are not withdrawal symptoms. Why does this matter? Actually, it matters a lot, because if you know you are not in withdrawal there would be no point smoking to relieve the symptoms, would there? Knowing that could make all the difference between staying stopped and starting again.

There is another thing that can make you feel strange when you stop smoking, and it's oxygen. You see, when you have a cigarette, about ten percent of the oxygen you normally have in your brain is pushed out and replaced by carbon monoxide from the tobacco smoke. Over the years your brain gets accustomed to working on this 90:10 mix. When you stop smoking, your brain has to adjust to 100% oxygen and during this period you can suffer from slight dizziness, which you could easily mistake for withdrawal symptoms. Two words of advice if this happens; first, don't make the mistake of thinking smoking would help, and second, don't stand on top of any tall buildings.

Seriously, if you find you are having quite severe mental symptoms which are resolved by a cigarette, try this little experiment instead of smoking. Breathe a few times into a bag. This will raise your carbon monoxide level, which will mimic what happens when you smoke. If it works, do this from time to time, until you no longer need it.

We sometimes tell patients that if they have one day of detox for each year they have smoked that would not be unreasonable, and they tend to agree, but in practice it rarely does take that long. The only exception I have noticed, in addition to my colleague Dr Freed's comments above, is that very occasionally a patient will develop an allergy, to anything, after stopping. This appears to be a reaction caused by the immune system being strengthened by stopping smoking. It's a paradox that hasn't, unfortunately, yet been properly researched.

And by the way, we sometimes have patients saying they have been told that stopping smoking, especially if you are a heavy smoker, can be a great strain on the body. Stuff and nonsense. Well, alright, there are major changes and the body will take some time to get used to not being abused, but that's the point. Not smoking can only ever be easier on your body than smoking, no matter how sudden the change.

What happens to you emotionally

So much for the physiological reaction to stopping, but what happens in your mind when you succeed? And that inevitably leads us to ask why so many people go back to smoking just when they think they have succeeded and they can stop worrying about it.

The first thing to recognise is that your brain is a physical organ. Quite apart from what you think with your brain, as a physical organ itself it has been suffering abuse all these years from your smoking. Can I say how much of what goes on at this stage is physiological in origin and how much is psychological? No. No-one can, because no-one has done the research, so the best I can give you is knowledge based on observation.

People's psychological reaction to stopping smoking

ranges from incredulousness that they've finally done it to trying to convince themselves that they will never keep it up. Almost everything you think when you do stop smoking is conditioned by the twin fears of failure and success, and that means you can still be afraid of failing, even though you have just succeeded, and you can still be afraid of succeeding, even though you have, as I said, just done it and the world didn't come to an end.

In other words, all the issues that affected you before you stopped smoking, the ones that made you afraid to try, and that made you give in when the going got tough, are still there after you succeed. The issues that make it hard to stop smoking are the same ones that make it hard to stay stopped, with one exception - you are no longer addicted to nicotine.

Not being addicted is great, but it often isn't enough. This is because addiction creates psychological dependence, remember. Once it has done that, paradoxically the dependence no longer needs the addiction. Tobacco can have almost as firm a grip on you after the addiction is over as before. Don't think it's going to let go of you just because you aren't addicted, oh no. It's like an alien in your brain controlling you, even after it's dead. (Listen, you let it in, remember.) Tobacco's job, once you have beaten it, is to win you back.

So what's the answer? How do you resolve the problem of this seemingly never-ending control? Well, the first thing to do it to recognise it for what it is, to understand that as soon as you stop smoking tobacco is going to try to make you start again. The second thing is to read Part One again, all of it if you have to, as soon as you have stopped smoking, to arm yourself against believing the wrong things. And the third thing is to turn to Project 12 in

Part Two and learn the Four Promises. And I do mean learn them, because I want you to have those promises in your head every waking minute. They are your unassailable armour against tobacco.

Most people feel good about stopping smoking, but I am going to make you a promise. You will, at some time, be challenged by the idea of smoking again. Once you stop, in fact the instant you stop, everything now is about staying stopped, and at the risk of repeating myself, understanding the issues I have been talking about in Part One is how you stay stopped (and I shall probably repeat this again, in the next tutorial even).

Fascinating Fact Number 11

Can you guess how much government funding there is in the UK each year for research into smoking cessation? Given that smoking is the largest cause of premature death in the country, just try to guess, to the nearest ten million, say, how much they spend.

The answer: nothing.

Use this space to make any comments or note any reminders for yourself.

Tutorial Twelve

Why ex-smokers start again, and how not to

I've got some good news and some bad news. The bad news first:

Once a smoker always someone who used to be a smoker. This means that for the rest of your life you are going to be vulnerable to starting again. The good news? It doesn't matter.

A little story:

A patient came to us and described a previous attempt to stop smoking. One day, he said, I was driving along a country road and it was lovely and sunny and I had the windows down and it felt pretty good. I reached for my cigarettes on the passenger seat but instead of lighting one I got a sudden urge not to do it and there and then I threw them away, just chucked them out of the window. I didn't smoke for a year after that.

Some time later a man came to the clinic and related

not how he had once stopped but why he had started again, a subject we always look into.

One day, he said, I was going for a walk in the country. As I walked alongside a country road this car came along and just as it passed me a pack of cigarettes and a lighter came flying out of the window and landed on the grass. It was like a sign from Heaven that I should smoke again.

Now you think I'm making this up, but the truth is sometimes stranger than fiction, because I'm not. I don't know if the two men did actually meet on the same country road, but I tell the story because it's lovely but also to illustrate just how easy it is to start again. If you have ever stopped smoking you know how true that is, don't you?

So, given that smokers stop for all the right reasons, and given that every ex-smoker I've ever spoken to says not smoking is better than smoking, why do so many start again? And the second question is, once they have started again why do so many find it hard to stop again? Wouldn't you think that if they had been happy non-smokers they would deal with it pretty quickly? Why don't they?

People who start smoking again almost all have one thing in common. They are surprised when they find they want to smoke. They thought they had won, and there they are, days, weeks or months later, and they want to smoke. And they interpret that wanting as meaning they must, so they do. There is lots to say about a different way to respond to the wanting, and I'll be doing that in Part Two, but for now it's enough to remember that once you have stopped you are, almost certainly, going to want to smoke at some time. If you accept that fact now, and get used to it, when it happens you are less likely to get caught out and more likely to follow the instructions I shall be giving you.

Wanting to smoke, once you have stopped, should not come as a surprise for the simple reason that it is so obviously predictable. I'm not being negative. I talk to some hypnotherapists who say oh no, once I've stopped someone smoking that's it, they will never think about it again. Really? When they see people smoking all around them? I don't think so. I think they may not want to smoke for a long time, but I also think they will one day get caught out by an inexplicable urge to do it. Understanding that is the best protection you can have against it.

You could almost argue that stopping smoking is irrelevant, that actually the only issue is staying stopped, because all smokers stop every day, when they go to sleep, and is it not true that all smokers start smoking again every day, in the morning? I don't know, but it's worth thinking about.

Aha, you say, but in the morning I haven't really stopped so it's not a valid question. Well, who is to say you haven't stopped? Excuse me, but what exactly does stopped mean?

A patient came to us once and stopped smoking. She went off to see her GP, who had been nagging her about her smoking but hadn't actually offered her any worthwhile help with it. She told him she had stopped and he expressed surprise and he said how long have you been stopped for and she said ten days and he laughed. Come back, he said, and tell me when you've been stopped a year. She was so upset she smoked again. Doctor one, patient nil. Had I ruled the world I would have taken his licence off him.

So to a clever dick GP stopping means a year, and to me it means overnight, but where does the truth lie? How do you know when you have succeeded? Well, an easy answer but not necessarily the right one is that if you are not smoking you don't smoke. Aha but, you say, I'm only not smoking for now, but I know I will in an hour's time.

Yes? Can you guarantee that? What if you have a heart attack and die in that time? Would that mean you died a smoker or a non-smoker? Well, you say, a smoker, because I didn't believe I had stopped before I died. Or, you might say, a non-smoker because when I put that last one out I promised myself that would be my last ever cigarette.

Confused? Even if you're not, I am. We have a joke in the Institute, that the last time you will ever smoke will be at the crematorium. It's not a very nice joke, and it's got nothing to do with the matter in hand, but I think it's funny so in it goes.

Anyway, why does all this stuff about success matter? It matters because smokers have difficulty believing in success.

Time and time again I talk with a patient we have helped and I say it's good isn't it, you've stopped smoking, and they say well, yes, for now, but who knows what will happen tomorrow or next week?

Excuse me? You do. You really think you don't know what you are going to do next week? I don't know what other people are going to do to me, but I do know what I am going to do. They talk as if smoking is something that happens to them, rather than something they do. They're talking as if it's something they have no control over, and remember they have just successfully stopped smoking. And that's the point. Smokers have this bizarre notion that smoking is something that happens to them. Right now, in the UK, there are perhaps at least fourteen million people who regret that they started smoking (even if they won't admit they want to stop). I suppose they could be forgiven for thinking that smoking is something that happens to them.

And ex-smokers spend their whole lives wondering if it will happen to them again. Well look here, smoking doesn't happen to you, alright? Whether you do it again is totally in your control. You might be influenced by things, in fact you will be influenced by things, and you can be sure I shall be talking about those things, but for now I want you to be in no doubt whatever who will be responsible if you start smoking again. You.

Oh dear oh dear, look, don't take it personally. I don't mean you're useless and you must blame yourself for your own weakness. What I mean is that you have more control than you think, and that's a good thing, because now what you're looking at is the fact that it is in your power to decide not to. There are things you can do to ensure that you don't ever start again.

For example, getting pregnant

Not all women stop smoking when they get pregnant, which is sad, even though a lot of those who don't stop do at least cut down. Of those who do stop, a lot start again after the birth, or when they finish breast-feeding. Why? Well the answer is in why they stopped in the first place. They stopped for the baby. That's done now, so it's alright to smoke again. They weren't stopping for themselves.

What is especially sad is that they don't see the pointlessness of starting again, that they can't say hold on, I don't smoke so why start again? The reason for this is that they don't believe they have stopped.

They have just held their smoking in abeyance while they have a baby. They have been smokers who aren't smoking. It's quite likely they have a partner who himself smoked through the pregnancy because he wasn't the one having the baby, and that was a constant reminder to her that smoking is normal but you can't do it while you're pregnant but only while you're pregnant.

Well, if they can't see it what can you do? You could say at least pregnancy is some kind of smoking cessation technique, but to be honest it's not something you can do for the rest of your life, is it? If you're a woman, I mean.

What does starting again mean?

You think it's a silly question, don't you? You think it's obvious. Well, it isn't. Let me give you a typical scenario:

You've been stopped for say three weeks (and by stopped I don't mean you're taking nicotine products) and it's going well and you go out with friends and one thing leads to another and you light a cigarette. Don't tell me you wouldn't do it because I won't believe you.

You think I haven't heard this a thousand times?

So there you are, with this cigarette in your hand and you light up and take a drag and ... what do you think will happen? Will you draw deeply and sigh contentedly and think, yes, this is what I've been missing? No, unlikely (not impossible, but unlikely). What will probably happen is that you will cough and feel a bit light-headed and think oh, this isn't very nice, and you will look at the cigarette and wonder why then you'll take another puff and it still won't be how you used to remember it and you will put it out.

At this point, your life is in the balance.

Some people will move on from there and never smoke again but what do you do? You ask your friend for another one. Now why would you do that? Why, when your experience has just shown that you didn't enjoy it, would you do it again? What is there in the human brain that has the ability to take information and deliberately reverse it? Well I'll tell you. It's exactly what happened when you started smoking all those years ago. Then, you tried one and it was horrible but instead of saying well it's horrible so I won't bother you said it's horrible so I'd better try harder to enjoy it because my fiends do it and they say it's nice. Or something like that, probably very like that, even if you didn't say it to yourself consciously.

Now, you smoke and it's not nice but your brain says hold on, that's not right, it use to be nice so I'd better do it again. And you do. You miss the point completely. Tobacco smoke is poisonous. When you inhale it you are supposed to reject it, only what you do now is refuse to believe the information you are getting and go back instead to the old days when you were addicted and were unable to tell the difference between good and bad, between safe and poisonous, and you convince yourself that if it tastes bad it's not because it is bad but because you are misreading it. It's a fatal mistake, and I do mean fatal.

So by the end of the evening you have smoked four cigarettes and now instead of tasting bad they are alright. Why? Because you have re-addicted yourself and, remember, the poisons in tobacco smoke can only taste nice once you are addicted.

Then you buy a pack so you can give four back to your friend and you smoke another one when you get home and in the morning you wake up with a hangover (alcohol and tobacco give you a worse hangover than alcohol alone) and a packet on the kitchen table with fifteen cigarettes in it. You are unhappy. Why did you do it? Actually, why you did it is not the big question right now. The big question is what are you going to do with the fifteen cigarettes in that pack?

And now you make another invalid decision, one that could very well change your life. You decide that since you've bought them it would be a shame not to smoke them. After all, they cost good money.

But there is another reason why you smoke them. It's because you believe you have now failed, that you have started smoking again. You say to yourself well I've smoked now so it doesn't matter if I carry on smoking. It's incredible but true that the human mind is capable of being that irrational. We have the biggest brain on the planet and there are moments when we are complete idiots. Excuse me but if not smoking for three weeks isn't success how come smoking five cigarettes is failure?

Which is better, not smoking for three weeks or smoking for one evening?

The point is that everyone knows that if you smoke you have failed. It's rubbish, but that doesn't stop everyone knowing it. So now you see the way out of this nonsense. You have to understand that smoking does not mean you have failed to stop smoking.

Look, let me give you an example:

You pass your driving test and you buy a car and for the next ten years you drive without incident. Then you have a prang. It's your fault, bang to rights, hands up, silly mistake, you got it wrong. It must mean you failed your driving test.

Well no, of course it doesn't. But when you stop smoking and then you have one, or even a whole pack, for some reason it means you failed to stop smoking.

A patient phoned us once and said hullo, I'm one of your failures. I came to you two years ago and I've just had a cigarette. Ho ho.

Smoking does not undo the success you had in stopping smoking. That success stands, whatever you subsequently do.

So let's go back to you in your kitchen and the fifteen cigarettes. You smoke one, it makes you feel a bit dizzy but actually that's quite a nice feeling if you look at it in a certain way, and then you put the pack in your pocket and go out. By the end of the day you have not only smoked them but you've also bought another pack. Well, you're going out tonight and now you've smoked what's the point of not enjoying smoking this evening?

Never mind that actually what you really enjoyed was the three weeks not smoking, and when you did smoke you didn't enjoy it, but you're not about to let those facts get in the way. You know you enjoy smoking. Alright, you have no evidence to back that up but you know it must be true because people say so, so you're going to smoke tonight.

And a year later you're thinking I really must do something about my smoking. Except that now you know you fail, because after all you failed a year ago, didn't you? There's always a reason not to stop again. What is so desperately sad is that you preferred it when you didn't smoke. What you have done is said to tobacco that you will allow it to control you again, and dictators all have one thing in common - if you give them control over you they don't let you take it back from them. You handed your life back to tobacco. You didn't intend to, but you did it all the same.

Case Study

Michael stopped easily enough. In fact he said he could hardly believe it was so easy after all the years of trying, it was like someone had given him his life back. At that point, what with him being so grateful, you would have put money on him never smoking again. You would have lost it.

We tell patients until we're blue in the face that smoking is never going to help them when they're stressed, and they nod and say oh no, I accept that completely, and then when they get stressed they smoke. Michael said it was stress, as if that was alright, as if he expected us to say oh, stressed, were you, well that explains it. Well, excuse me, if everyone who is stressed starts smoking again they are all doomed, because as sure as eggs is eggs they are all going to come under stress.

The problem wasn't that Michael actually believed smoking was relieving his stress. After all, he was just as stressed with it as without it, and he knew that. The problem was that his brain was hardwired to smoke when he was stressed, not listen to logic. His brain was simply incapable of rational thought when he got stressed. Appealing to his intelligence was pointless, because smokers hand their intelligence over to the tobacco companies when they sign up.

On the intellectual level Michael knew what was going on, but on the emotional level he was putty in their hands. He had no power to resist them. He could have a cigarette in his hand while he was saying this isn't helping, but carry on smoking it. He would know, while he was doing it, that it made no sense, but he couldn't stop doing it. If you have any doubts at all about the awesome power of tobacco, this is what it's capable of. Tobacco can make you say black is white and white is black, know you're wrong, despise yourself for saying it, but say it all the same.

Michael was desperate. We were not a little otherwise ourselves. Our work is largely predicated on logical argument - tell the patient the facts and he will use them to save his life. You might have noticed that, reading this Handbook.

So what, you're wondering, was the answer? The answer was that the fear of stopping smoking, believe it or not, stays with some people after they have actually stopped. The fear of most things goes away with actual experience of that thing, but with smoking the brain is so much under the control of the drug that even after you stop using it the fear of coming off it can remain. When you then start smoking again it does a terrible thing - it confirms in your brain that you shouldn't have stopped in the first place, that the fear was justified. And if you were afraid to stop before, now you have started again you find it almost impossible to think straight. Which means there is no cognitive approach that will work.

In Michael's case, we were considering using hypnotherapy to overcome the problem, to help us bypass the fear by getting straight into his subconscious mind, but in the end we didn't need to. Our resident homeopath gave him a remedy that worked directly on the problem medically, and within a week Michael's attitude to stopping had changed dramatically. We put him back on the original treatment we had used for him to stop, and he simply stopped smoking.

Now let's look at how this might all have gone so differently.

You were tempted to smoke, but why? You could have thought about that at the time and decided not to, but you didn't. You could have said to your friends at the beginning of the evening don't offer me a cigarette and if I ask for one be as rude as you like but don't give me one. In other words, you could have built in a safety net, but you didn't. When you smoked the first cigarette you could have thought blimey this is horrible, I won't do it any more, but you didn't. Before you lit the next one you could have thought back to the first one and decided it's not what you want and it makes no sense to do it again, but you didn't. Before you bought a pack you could have given your friend the money instead of buying some to give him a few back, but you didn't. When you got home you could have thought how much you regretted buying them and thrown them away, but you didn't. In the morning ditto, but you didn't. And so on, and on, for another year.

You see, when you make the mistake and smoke there is nothing inevitable about the next stage, nothing that says at this point you have become a smoker again, because if you stop and think, if you have a structure to adhere to, if you stop behaving like a robot programmed by the tobacco companies, there is one opportunity after another to deal with it. But you don't. Well, carry on like that if you like but on the other hand maybe not. Maybe now it's time to change.

Now you've learned about how to start smoking again and how not to, this is the last tutorial in Part One. The practical side of not starting again is addressed in the last project in Part Two, which is where it belongs, but you will be going through all the other projects before you get to that.

Use this space to make any comments or note any reminders for yourself.

PART TWO

The Projects

Project One

Find out if you really want to do this

You're not sure, are you? You are? OK, prove it. Do these simple tests.

The one-minute motivation test

Question: If your fairy godmother could wave a magic wand and turn the clock back so you had never started smoking, would you want that?

Yes ☐ No ☐

If you answered no, forget all about ever stopping smoking.

If you answered Yes, you want to be someone who doesn't smoke. Your problem is not BEING a non-smoker but BECOMING one. You've got so hung up on the stopping bit, you've lost sight of the pleasure of the being bit.

From now on, never forget you want to be a non-smoker, and never allow yourself to doubt your motivation.

The two-minute enjoyment test

In case you still think you enjoy smoking, do this test. Buy a brand of cigarettes you don't normally smoke, but with a similar tar/nicotine content. If you don't enjoy it, then you have just proved you don't enjoy smoking. What you enjoy is the fix - your enjoyment is drug specific and has nothing to do with the delivery method. And for most smokers that is even brand-specific.

The NSCI lie detector test

If you believe you want to be a non-smoker, do this simple test now. Imagine that the government, bless it, has been secretly researching how to genetically modify tobacco plants so that cigarettes can be made from them that are almost completely safe to smoke.

The new tobacco is about to be launched commercially and the government, bless it, has announced that it wants everyone to change over to it, so they are not going to tax it, at all, so in the UK twenty cigarettes will cost, say, a pound. What's more, these new cigarettes will actually smell quite pleasant, so people won't even mind if you smoke in their homes.

Try to imagine all of this is true. Now, you can smoke with a completely clear conscience, with no health worries, or financial or social issues either. Would you:

Still stop smoking ☐ Try them for a while ☐

If you would still want to stop, then yes, you really do want to stop smoking. If, though, you admit you would try the new cigarettes first before deciding, you don't really. You just don't want to pay the price (in the fullest sense) of smoking, which is not the same thing at all. Many patients in our clinics, when we ask them this question, say they would put the programme on hold and try the new cigarettes first.

If this is you it doesn't mean you don't want to be a non smoker. It does mean, though, that you need to revisit your reasons for stopping. You want to stop because of the negative issues around smoking, not because you just don't want to smoke any longer.

Does this mean you're a hopeless case? Would I have put you through this exercise just to prove you won't succeed? Of course not. I did it to expose the reality you have to face. I could almost say you're stopping smoking for the wrong reasons (but I wouldn't, because they're all good reasons even so), and I want you to learn something from this test, which is that you want to carry on smoking but can't. With that understanding, you will accept the work you still have to do. I could say that you need to change your attitude. Come to think of it, I will. You need to change your attitude.

And finally:

The I've failed so I can't stop so I don't want to stop test

An awful lot of people we talk to say they don't want to stop, and then when we question them further they say they've tried, lots of times, and this raises an interesting question, which I want you to answer now.

How many attempts, serious or otherwise, have you made to stop smoking:

1 ☐ 2 ☐ 3 ☐ 4 ☐ More ☐

Although obviously the more attempts you have made the more it means you want to stop, if you have made any attempts at all it completely negates any statement you might make to the effect that you don't want to stop. Why on Earth would you have tried to stop if you don't want to?

Your problem is not that you don't want to stop, it's that you've failed, perhaps many times, so you no longer believe you can. That's not the same thing at all, and I want you to promise me, right now, that you will stop believing this nonsense.

What do you think you've learned from this project?
Are there any Tutorials you need to re-read as a result?

Project Two

Test the incorrect beliefs that keep you smoking

In this project you are going first to complete the questionnaire before reading any of Part One, then you are going to come back to it after reading the whole of Part One and completing the first two Projects. Why? Well, you'll see.

Tick the reasons, in column A, that you can't stop smoking:

	A	B	C	D
Stress				
Boredom				
Social/drinking				
Addiction				
Not sure you want to				
You enjoy it				

Now, put a number in column B that places these reasons in order of importance. Don't put anything in the other columns. That's it. Now you can go back and start Part One.

A week later ......

Alright, now you've read all of Part One and I'm hoping you've changed rather a lot of your ideas. It's time to come back to our list of perceived problems above and tick some more boxes. Do the same as last time: tick in column C any box you feel represents a problem for you, and then put them in order in column D.

Don't put what you think I would want you to say, just be honest.

OK. Are columns C and D different from columns A and B?

If they're not, either I haven't explained things very well or you are determined to prove me a liar, in which case this is where we part company.

Assuming there has been a change, think about this change. Think about the fact that before you started this Handbook you couldn't stop smoking because you didn't understand what the problems really were, and now you do. That, in fact, has been the whole point of the exercise. It's why you bought this Handbook. Actually, you probably bought the Handbook because you thought it was going to give you some magic formula that would stop you smoking without having to think about it. Well, it's too late to get your money back now.

Seriously, haven't you just proved that you got it wrong before but now you know how to fix it? A bit at least?

Think about the Project you have just completed, and write down your thoughts on what you have learned so far. Do you think the way you have changed is going to help you to stop smoking?

Project Three

Assess why you can't stop

If you have learned anything thus far from this Handbook, I hope it is that you have failed to stop smoking because you have been doing it wrong. Failure to achieve something is usually because you do it wrong, so why should stopping smoking be any different?

You have almost certainly also started to understand your past mistakes, and hopefully you have made a commitment not to make them again. But let's go further, let's analyse what you did and why it didn't work. We go through this kind of procedure in our clinical programme, Phoenix (because it's a long consultation and we have time to do it, and anyway it's a fundamental of medical practice, for us at least, that we can't help a patient until we understand them). You can't decide what to do in future until you know what was wrong with the past, can you?

This project is also rather similar to the workshops we run for corporate clients. I have a great time standing in front of a group of smokers writing all this stuff on a whiteboard and watching their little faces as the lights start to come on in their heads. There are two parts to it.

The first is going to help you to understand your individual problems with stopping smoking and in the second you will see why the attempts you made failed, because they failed to address the reasons you can't stop.

Let me give you an example. A smoker goes on a nicotine replacement product, for the simple reason that her GP gives it to her. The GP might have no idea why she can't stop and what this product might do to resolve that problem, and neither might she, but that issue never arises in the consultation. She takes the product and lo and behold for a few days she doesn't smoke. This looks good. Then, the threat to her job becomes real and she is made redundant. Guess what? Yes, she starts smoking again. She does that because she believes it's an appropriate response to her stress. It doesn't help of course, because her employer doesn't say, oh, you're a smoker, here's your job back. She stops using the NRP and smokes instead, because she is responding to a different problem from the one the NRP is supposed to address (which is the habit of smoking). It's a classic case of trying to solve the wrong problem, and if we've seen it once we've seen it a thousand times, and I'm not exaggerating.

Enough with the introduction already, so here goes. You have already done Project 2, twice; once before reading the tutorials in Part One, and again since, and I hope and trust that there has been a difference, that you can now see how just thinking the wrong things has got you into trouble.

What you are going to do now, with this new knowledge, is to ask yourself some searching questions. First, I want you to write down the list, from Project 2, that you ticked in column A, the reasons you can't stop smoking. This means the reasons you gave before you started reading the Handbook. You may not believe those things now but I want to look at you when you did believe them. Write each reason in a box here on the left:

Now, I want you to put in the right-hand boxes a list of the methods you have used to try and stop smoking. Just the methods, not 'cold turkey', because turkeys are not a method. For each 'problem', I want you to write the exact same list of 'solutions', even though this will mean repeating yourself.

At any stage, I want you to feel free, when you read in this Handbook about the various smoking cessation methods, to return to this project and look at the method you tried and failed with, and I want you to ask yourself a question.

Did you fail, or did the method fail you, BECAUSE IT WAS THE WRONG THING TO DO?

Think about your previous attempts to stop.
Can you see now where you were going wrong,
and how different it is now going to be?

Project Four

Tailor the plan to your personal needs

You should by this stage have discovered why you have failed to stop smoking, so by my reckoning you are now half way towards successfully stopping. This project and the ones that follow it are all concerned with preparing to stop, finding the right help if you need it, and stopping and staying stopped. You have been patient to have come this far, for which I thank you, but now you are going into the second half of the process of stopping.

There are three possibilities from this point on. Which one applies to you?

- You have found the Handbook so inspiring that you are going, with the help of the following projects, to stop smoking without any further assistance.

- You are going to use a non-NSCI product or service to help you, or you are already using one.

- You have been given this Handbook as part of a programme from the Institute.

You should use only the relevant part of this project.

Stopping with the Handbook on its own

Obviously, if you are already in one of the Institute's programmes, or you are already using a drug product, this doesn't apply, but if you are not let's look at trying to stop without them.

An enormous amount of research has gone into what you are reading in this Handbook, starting in 1991, with tens of thousands of smokers. It is based on one question - why can't people stop smoking? Our research is unusual in the medical world, in that instead of looking for answers, and then for problems those answers might apply to (like developing a drug and then looking for a disease it might cure), which is the norm in the pharmaceutical industry, we don't look for any answers at all until we have asked questions. Learning to ask questions is in fact a fundamental, we believe, of research.

The Handbook is the answer to the questions we have been asking, but it is not a solution on a plate for you. If you work with it with the correct attitude (remember attitudes?) you are going to learn a lot, enough perhaps to succeed.

If you have a serious history of failure you might need help, you might need to buy a product or join a programme, and to be honest I think not a few of the smokers who come to us could have done it on their own, if they had had this Handbook for example, but they pay for our help because it's easier than struggling, and who am I to say they are wrong? They, after all, are the people who teach us everything we know, and to be blunt they provide the income that supports our research.

If you were just fortunate enough to come by this Handbook, have a go. Don't spend money you don't need to spend, but there is another reason. I believe, from years of experience, that the people who do best are those who make a personal commitment, who are prepared to learn how to help themselves.

Anyway, enough of that. You should now turn to the next project and complete all the other projects in Part Two, except for Project 11. If you subsequently do use a drug product or an NSCI programme, you will need to come back to the relevant part of this project, but let's hope you don't need to.

Stopping with a non-NSCI product or service

This includes all of the drug products prescribed by GPs and over-the-counter drugs bought from pharmacists, so we're talking about every nicotine replacement product as well as the psychotropic drugs GPs prescribe, currently Zyban and Champix / Chantix. I don't differentiate between NRPs generally, unless there is a specific reason to, because they all work in the same way.

Nicotine replacement products

The function of all nicotine replacement products is to

give you enough nicotine to prevent withdrawal symptoms, while you break the habit of lighting cigarettes. NRPs are specifically a habit-breaking tool.

There are some general reasons I can give why people fail on these products, and some suggestions as to what you might do about this. In addition, you can consult your GP, the pharmacist you bought the products from, or the NHS smoker's helpline.

The product is too difficult to use

There might be a number of difficulties:

- Some users find the gum unpleasant to taste, and it can cause stomach upsets. It's hard to chew with false teeth.

- The patch sometimes causes a reaction, which might be to the plaster or the nicotine itself.

- The inhalator can cause an unpleasant burning sensation in the throat.

It seems pretty obvious that if you have a problem with one product you might try a different kind.

You still crave a cigarette

Some users get satisfaction from nicotine with NRPs and some don't. It is not understood why there is a difference but we believe from our research that it is largely psychological.

Tick here if you have craved while using the product

You complete the course but start smoking again immediately afterwards

This is obviously because as long as you are getting nicotine you don't need to smoke, and what that means is the reason you can't stop is the addiction to nicotine. In your case, it doesn't matter how you get the drug, from an NRP or a cigarette. The NRP at least serves a useful function, because it shows you what the problem is.

Tick here if this has happened to you

Some people use the nicotine gum for a very long time, transferring their dependence from cigarettes onto it, and I'm talking about years. A word about this. Don't. It is contraindicated and the manufacturers do warn about this.

If you have been on nicotine gum for years, think of yourself as having the same health risks as a long-term smoker, and do something about it. (The Institute has programmes to bring you off the gum.)

Psychotropic drugs

The purpose of psychotropic drugs like those used in smoking cessation is to alter your brain chemistry, on the assumption that your brain might reject the signals of withdrawal it is getting if it is on a high.

Like all drugs, they should be treated with some caution.

We get people phoning us complaining that their GP won't prescribe them, and our advice to them is to listen to their doctor, who is likely to know something about the risks involved with taking drugs to stop smoking. If you have any mental health issue, or are already on an antidepressant drug, these are contraindicated, as they are also in pregnancy.

If your GP refuses to prescribe these drugs, then accept they are not for you. There are many contraindications and your GP knows best. If you are tempted to use some prescribed for someone else, or to buy them on the Web, don't.

If you are on Zyban or Champix, your GP or the practice nurse will be monitoring you for reactions, and therefore you will be under constant care and can talk with them about any issues around stopping smoking. If you have not yet started taking the drug, it would be sensible to try stopping with the Handbook first, but if you really do need more help, how should you use the Handbook and the drug together?

I'm inclined to defer to your medical advisor on this one, because they are the one putting you on the drug. Read the whole of Part One, but then show them the Handbook and ask for their advice about Part Two.

Using hypnotherapy or acupuncture or any other service independently of the NSCI

If you are going to see a hypnotherapist or an acupuncturist, or if you are booked to do the Allen Carr's Easyway session, following the Handbook will supplement those. Some of what is in it will conflict with what you are told in Easyway; Allen Carr formulated his opinions about smoking many years ago and I am not going to criticise them.

The Handbook is based on the latest research available, so look at it as an update on what the Easyway people tell you.

If you have seen a non-NSCI hypnotherapist or acupuncturist, and you subsequently came across the Handbook, then either you don't need any further help or, more likely since you bought the Handbook, things have not gone according to plan, in which case follow the whole of it as if you were stopping with no other help.

Having said that, if you made any progress at all with either therapy, and I include stopping even for one day, don't dismiss that as failure. Build on the work you have done so far.

Using the Handbook as part of a programme from the National Smoking Cessation Institute

The literature you have received with the Handbook will tell you which programme you are in. Whichever it is, the Handbook is no longer a plan to stop smoking, it is background reading for the programme. Use the Handbook according to the programme you are in, as described here.

The Phoenix Programme

You will have been sent the Handbook before attending your clinic appointment. You should read all of Part One, and you should do the following projects only:

Project 1
Project 2
Project 3
Project 6
Project 7

At this point you will attend the clinic and the advice you will receive there will supersede any further projects.

NSCI Hypnotherapy or NSCI Acupuncture

You should of course read all of Part One, and then do the following projects:

Project 1
Project 2
Project 3
Project 6
Project 8
Project 9
Project 11
Project 12

Because you are now in NSCI QuitClub, you have indefinite access to an NSCI counsellor for telephone support, so although you will do Project 12, it is QuitClub that you will now call for support if something goes wrong.

N5 Smoking Reduction Programme

This is the Institute's specialist programme for heavier

smokers who are going to use our help to become light smokers. Read only Part One, because none of Part Two applies to you. Your NSCI counsellor will give you projects to do that supersede all the projects in the Handbook.

The Epsilon Project

This is the Institute's research project. If you have been accepted onto Epsilon, you should treat the whole of the Handbook, in conjunction with the epsilon workbook, as your personal project, but of course you will also be working with the Epsilon team as instructed.

NSCI corporate programmes

If you are an employee of a client for whom we are running a Smokers' Workshop, read the whole of Part One, and follow the workshop leader's instructions from there.

Now make a note of what product or service you are going to use to stop smoking, and WHY.

Project Five

Work out if you need help and where to get it

You might just have bought this Handbook, or some lovely person gave it to you, and you want to stop but you really don't know what would be the right way to go about it. Can I offer you some guidance about choosing a smoking cessation product or programme?

Not easily, no, because to be honest I don't know you. When a smoker calls us we spend perhaps fifteen minutes on the phone talking about their problems with stopping before we feel we can make a recommendation. But since you have read this far it seems only fair to have a bash, so with your help here goes. Answer the questions here about your previous attempts to stop.

You haven't tried

If you have never tried to stop you should continue working through the Handbook. If you succeed, that's great. If you don't, at the very least you will have a far better idea why you can't stop than you did before and what the best approach would be for your personal circumstances.

You tried on your own

This is usually called cold turkey, but what turkeys, regardless of their temperature, have to do with stopping smoking is a mystery to me.

Did you stop, completely, for a week or more?

If you did, you have proved you can stop.

Have you done it more than once?

If not, you have done what a lot of smokers do. You have convinced yourself you failed. Actually, you didn't fail, you succeeded and then you went back to smoking, which is different, and if you can make yourself believe this there is no reason why, with the help of the Handbook, you shouldn't succeed again.

If you have succeeded several times, in other words you stop and start regularly, you are almost there. Perhaps with the help of the Handbook you will now stop for ever, but if not consider joining the Institute's research project, epsilon.

What you don't need is to be spending a lot of money or taking drugs to do what you have already proved you can do without them.

You had hypnotherapy
How it works

As you have read, when you become addicted to a drug that drug makes you dependent psychologically on the delivery method for the drug. With smoking, you become convinced you cannot stop. A good hypnotherapist can get into the dark recesses of your brain and implant ideas that you can stop, that you really do want to stop, and there is no reason why you won't succeed.

Some smokers might wonder, if addiction is as important in smoking as I have been saying (and it is), how hypnotherapy, which is a psychological therapy, can help to overcome it. It can. If you see a hypnotherapist who tries to convince you that addiction doesn't matter, I'm afraid they are improperly trained. Their job is to help your brain to overcome the addiction by disregarding the withdrawal symptoms. And if they want to take you back through your relationship with your father they are probably straying into areas of your psychology that are none of their business.

Most hypnotherapists do either one or two sessions.

Did you stop, completely, for a week or more?

If you did, use the Handbook to understand why you went back to smoking, and seriously consider using hypnotherapy again, either through the NSCI or with a non-NSCI therapist.

If you didn't, don't spend more money on it.

You did Allen Carr's Easyway session
How it works

The late Allen Carr ran a personal (and business) crusade to convince people they don't need to smoke. He wrote many books (none of them, of course, as good as this one) and started a national chain of franchises to preach the message.

The session lasts four hours, with a largish group usually, in which the leader talks you through the philosophy in the books.

Did you stop at the time, for at least a week? ☐
If not did you go back and fail again? ☐
Or did you go back and succeed? ☐

We see quite a lot of people who did this session, and most of them say it was good. Some liked it but didn't stop, some actually stopped for a while and started again. Why is this?

The programme is based on brainwashing. It's quite good at moving the client towards stopping, but seems to offer less in terms of the longer-term issues. And because it's brain-washing, if you start smoking again and go back and do it again, people tell us it often doesn't help the second time. I don't know if the company have figured out why, but we assume it's simply because the brain computes it is being washed and rejects the message. It's like a magic trick; once you've seen how it's done, it's no longer magic.

If you liked the session, consider hypnotherapy this time. If you didn't get on with it at all, ask yourself why, and then decide.

You had acupuncture
How it works

Acupuncture is a physical treatment and it therefore tackles the addiction itself, although some acupuncturists will broaden the treatment to incorporate detoxification and other health issues.

The principle is that acupuncture can relieve the pain and stress of withdrawal symptoms, leaving you more in control. It does this very well, but on its own it has limitations (which is why we always combine it with a psychological programme).

Acupuncture is actually very effective generally (I had it once, not for smoking, and it was amazing), and it has a lot to offer smokers, but we find that most acupuncturists simply aren't trained sufficiently to help smokers so they either don't offer help or they do so ineffectually. It's why we provide continuing professional development for them specifically to help smokers.

Did you stop smoking for at least a week? ☐
Did it do nothing to help? ☐

If you stopped for at least a week, I would certainly recommend doing it again.

You smoked herbal cigarettes
How they work

They are the opposite of NRPs. Nicotine replacement products give you nicotine without having to smoke for it, so they are a habit-breaking tool. Herbal cigarettes give you smoking without having to take nicotine at the same time, so their benefit is that they support you psychologically while you break the addiction to nicotine. For this reason, we put herbal cigarettes and NRPs much on a par in terms of effectiveness.

When people fail to stop smoking with herbal cigarettes, that is largely because they don't know what they're for and do it all wrong which, if you remember, I said right at the beginning is the main reason people fail generally.

You found them too unpleasant to smoke ☐
You thought they were alright but other people disliked the smell ☐
They helped you to stop for a while ☐

If you couldn't get on with one flavour, try another. The menthol, even if you don't normally smoke menthol, seems to be the easiest to smoke. If other people didn't like the smell, who cares?

Now I'll tell you how to use them. First, get down to the Addiction Threshold with the help of the Handbook. Now, if you roll your own, mix some Honeyrose herbal rolling mixture with your tobacco. Get used to the taste, and when you're ready switch to the herbal mixture alone. At this point you will be breaking the addiction to nicotine but because you are 'smoking' your brain will try to believe it doesn't matter. It's not foolproof, but it's definitely worth a try.

If you smoke ready-mades, get down to the Addiction Threshold, then try the Smoke-Free Day in Project 9, and then follow the instructions in Project 10.

In fact herbal cigarettes can be used to support any number of methods for stopping smoking. Say you have had hypnotherapy and you are smoking one or two cigarettes a day. Well, try switching these to herbals. A lot of people on NRPs still smoke, but actually this is an ideal situation in which to smoke herbals, because if you are getting nicotine from the NRP you shouldn't need tobacco - you just want the comfort of smoking something.

You used a nicotine replacement product
How they work

The function of an NRP is to give you nicotine without having to smoke. The reason for this is a little hazy. The manufacturers say this will help you to break the addiction for nicotine, but there seems to be a lack of science behind this claim. The most obvious benefit of using an NRP is that it helps you to break the habit of smoking which, if habit is the problem, might be helpful. There is no difference in the biochemical effect between types of NRP or brand.

The most common reaction to failing to stop with an NRP is to try another NRP. This isn't quite as daft as it sounds, but almost. Daft because if taking nicotine doesn't stop you smoking taking nicotine another way is unlikely to be an intelligent approach to the real reasons you can't stop. Shoving it into your body through any orifice in a desperate attempt to get a fix is not the kind of behaviour we encourage.

And not completely daft because it depends why you don't succeed with any given NRP. Answer these questions:

If you used gum:

Did you find it hard to chew, or unpleasant in any way?
Did it fail to satisfy your craving?

If you didn't like using it, the answer is that you don't know if taking nicotine will help you to stop smoking, so in this case it might be worth trying to get the nicotine another way.

If you used patches:

Did you find they slipped off/you reacted to the plaster?

Did they fail to satisfy your craving?

If there was a problem in use, again you never got to the point of learning if nicotine might help you to stop smoking, so try another product.

If you used the inhaler:

Did you find it unpleasant and hard to suck on?
Was it alright in use, but didn't satisfy the craving?

Here we go again. Yes, if you couldn't use it, try another product.

And so on. Another question:

You used an NRP satisfactorily, there were no problems and it satisfied the craving so you didn't smoke. But after a while, and especially if you tried coming off it, the craving simply came back and you smoked again?

The problem here was that taking nicotine satisfied your

need for nicotine (which when you think about it it should), but coming off the nicotine had the predictable result. In other words, because you were addicted to nicotine your body didn't care where you got the fix from, a cigarette or an NRP, but it insists that you get it from somewhere.

Does this mean using the NRP was a waste of time and money? No, because it taught you something very important - that your problem is addiction to nicotine (which of course you won't break taking more nicotine).

All of which leaves an important question, and it's one that comes up time and time again with our patients, practically all of whom have used NRPs before they come to us. A lot of them report they still wanted to smoke even using the NRP. They not unnaturally assumed this was because they had a psychological need for a burning cigarette in their hand. It's a nice theory, but it's not true. You could hold a burning cigarette in your hand, while you chew nicotine gum or suck a nicotine lozenge. You could even smoke a herbal cigarette while you use an NRP.

The answer is another question:

When you smoke a cigarette you get nicotine. Is this nicotine:

Raw? ☐ Burned? ☐

If you answered raw, go to the back of the class. You have to burn tobacco to smoke it, and you are therefore addicted to burned nicotine. Raw nicotine has an entirely different chemical structure and unless you habitually chew the stuff your body doesn't know what to do with it.

So unless the NRP is made from burned nicotine, it is not presenting the chemical information to your body in a form that will give you a fix. Ask your doctor or pharmacist if the NRP they are putting you on is made from burned nicotine.

You took a psychotropic drug
How they work

They do approximately what hypnotherapy does, but they do it chemically.

This means Zyban (buproprion hydrochloride) or Champix (Chantix in the United States), or any other drug marketed between me writing this and you reading it. If you had a bad reaction to the drug, then it is not for you and you need to look at some other method. These products, being drugs of last resort, will not have been prescribed by your GP unless they had already tried to help you with nicotine replacement products, so at this point you have reached the end of the road as far as taking drugs to stop smoking is concerned.

If you have been given this Handbook as part of one of the Institute's programmes, then obviously you have already sorted out how you are going to stop.

Some futurology

Drug companies would love to create a vaccine for nicotine (largely because they perceive the neutrogen we use as a vaccine, which it actually isn't) and several of them are currently working on one. The problem they have is that you can't create a vaccine for a poison. Vaccines are for viruses and bacteria, and nicotine is obviously neither, so how can they resolve this problem?

Our understanding is that they have genetically modified the cholera bacterium to get it to absorb a molecule of nicotine. This, they theorise, will, if injected into the body, stimulate the production of antibodies to the combined bacterium/poison. If they succeed it will be a considerable scientific achievement.

It is hard to see what the point would be, though. The theory is that this 'vaccine', when injected, would confer immunity to tobacco, and they will want therefore to inject children with it to prevent them liking tobacco if they try smoking it. The point is, though, that children DON'T like tobacco when they first smoke it. This is because tobacco is poisonous - and the body is born with a natural immunity to poisons.

The pursuit of profit is all very well, but is this science gone mad?

Something you haven't done

The Institute's Phoenix Programme is possibly new to you. As a not-for-profit organisation, we don't promote it, and you certainly haven't bought this Handbook to be sold a programme (although we might have given it to you because you are already in one of our programmes, including Phoenix).

If you have a history of failure, you can get some information about Phoenix by contacting us. See 'Where to get help' at the back of the Handbook or visit the Institute's website.

Phoenix is available only in the UK for the foreseeable future.

Time for a scrupulously honest assessment of why you have failed before. Now, write down, based on this project and the previous one, what your new plan of action is.

Project Six

Eliminate the things that might trip you up

There are three things that might trip you up while you try to stop smoking, or once you have stopped:

Tobacco You Other people

What you are going to do in this project is to analyse why each of these might be a problem and decide what to do about it.

The key to all of this, of course, is you. Neither tobacco nor other people can make you do what you don't want to do. It's your life, and it's your mouth and you can decide what you put in it. So, first, write in the box here what you think your weaknesses are.

If you've written I'm pathetic, cross that out. This is not an exercise in self-pity. Now, in the next box, write down your strengths, the good things you are going to be bringing to this.

It's a smaller box, isn't it? We have to face the truth.

Now, in this next box, I want you to write down your thoughts on tobacco, and the tobacco industry, from the manufacturers to the shop you buy it from and the government that is part of the tobacco business because it taxes it. What control does tobacco have over you?

So much for you and your relationship with tobacco. What about other people? Who are the people who are going to help you and which ones are going to be a problem? The government, bless it, produces those leaflets, you know, the ones with the silly cartoons and stuff on it that you already know, and one of the bits of really helpful advice they give is choose a buddy to stand by you. Well, that, apparently, is the cutting edge of the government's, bless it, smoking cessation technology.

First, split people into smokers and non-smokers. The non-smokers are generally going to be encouraging or, at worst, disinterested. The ex-smokers among them are likely to give you all sorts of advice based on their own experience and I can tell you now that most of it will be unhelpful so try not to take any notice of it. No-one knows as much about stopping as an ex-smoker, and funnily enough the way they did it, which they will tell you all about whether you want to hear it or not, is not only the best way but the only way to do it. My advice is to avoid those conversations like the plague.

The smokers will themselves split into two groups, those who are helpful and those who aren't. The ones who encourage you are hoping you will do it so they don't have to, because this will assuage their conscience for carrying on. And then you get the unhelpful ones. Why are they unhelpful? Well, mostly, sadly, because they feel threatened by you stopping.

A smoker can be like an alcoholic, happy only with other alcoholics because people who don't drink embarrass people who do. This camaraderie a lot of smokers think exists among smokers is nothing more than smokers protecting each other from having to face the truth. If you stop you are a deserter.

My advice is not to talk about it with these people. How do you do that? You can of course avoid them for a while, until you've stopped for sure and are less vulnerable to their goading. Or, if that's not easy, you can simply play down the stopping thing. I've known lots of people whose own families don't even notice that they're not smoking any more.

The worst smoker is the one who tells you you've failed before so you're bound to fail this time. Not only is it patently not true because what has the past to do with the future, but really, what is the point of saying it? In what way is it meant to be helpful? Of course, that's the point, it's not.

Now I come to your close family and perhaps your partner, and everything I've said so far applies because they might be smokers or non-smokers or ex-smokers, but if they are really close they have a stronger influence on you. I'm less concerned here with the people who are going to help you, which is all very nice, than the people who are going to hinder you.

Believe me I hear people who simply push someone to smoke again. They're out there. They should be put up against a wall and shot, but sadly I don't run the country so they get away with it. If you know anyone like that, you must avoid them. I don't want to hear pathetic excuses about not wanting to upset them. Write in this next box anyone who must be avoided at all costs.

It's a small box because I'm hoping there aren't many of them. You must make a commitment now, not because you hate these people but because you know they are dangerous, that you will have nothing to do with them while you stop smoking. What if your partner is on this list though? Leave them.

Alright, maybe not. In which case you have no choice but to talk this through with them. A smoking partner is a problem. I see patients who say oh no, he'll be fine, he's promised to support me with this, and I say so he won't be smoking in the house, and she says well no, I can't ask him to do that, can I? Well excuse me, what exactly is this support we're talking about that doesn't extend to not smoking in front of you?

Come on people, this is not a game. Oh well, they say, he'll smoke in the garden. Yes, and you will stand in the kitchen watching him wondering how come he's allowed to smoke and you're not. I don't think so. Sorry folks, but support means not smoking at home, period. If that is too much to ask, and you are coming off a drug that kills 300 people a day, you need to ask some serious questions. Like what would you do if I needed you to donate a kidney to save my life? Well, I would do it because I love you. Thank you darling. And what would you do if I was drowning? I would jump in and save you, of course. Thank you darling. What would you do if I needed you to not smoke anywhere near our home?

I think I may have made my point.

So what this project is about is removing yourself from the way of harm and setting up people around you who are going to give you the right help. Telling friends not to offer you cigarettes, even if you beg, telling your local tobacconist not to sell you any, even if you think that's crazy; in short, not sabotaging yourself. By the time you finish reading this you are going to be taking this whole thing very much more seriously. You are going to be ready to go into the next project with a grim determination that you are not going to stumble at the first hurdle, because this matters, really matters, to you.

List here the obstacles that have been a problem before. Think particularly about people who colluded in your failure, even if they didn't mean to.

Project Seven

Deal with stress before you stop

As you've read, stress (including physical stress, as in withdrawal) is the single most important reason why people fail to stop smoking, and why they start again when they have stopped. I won't rehearse the reasons why, which you now understand.

So is it going to have this effect on you? Yes. Look, just reading all this common-sense stuff isn't going to change anything, because when people get stressed they don't listen to common sense, and if your reaction to stress in the past has been drug-taking that is exactly what you will do in future.

That's the bad news. The good news is that it's not true. Or at least it doesn't have to be. No, I'm not saying you should be less stressed, because strange as it may seem I accept you would if you could. If you can't change the stressors in your life, though, you can change your reaction to them, and that's what you are going to get to grips with now.

Actually, you are going to do two things in this project:

- You are going to learn to alter your stress reaction.
- You are going to break the connection between stress and smoking.

Of course you might not, but let's have a go anyway. But even before that I want to do something else. I am not a believer that you can, with the right 'expert' help, have a less stressful life, and if I tried I would be a terrible example because to be honest it has not been easy for me either but you don't want to know about me.

The stress barrel

Having said that, the bit about not being able to change the stressors in your life, no, perhaps not, but actually there is a very interesting little exercise I learned from the same Dr Richard Mackarness who got me involved in the business of smoking cessation. He argued that the reason people are unable to change the stressors in their life is because they do it the wrong way (sound familiar?). People become obsessed with the big stressors and get overwhelmed by them, which I suppose is fair enough, that's human nature, but he proposed a different way of looking at it. As he was, among other things, a consultant psychiatrist he probably knew what he was talking about.

This is what you do. Below, you will see a barrel. Think of this as the sum total of all your stressors. Everything that is currently adding to your stress load is in this barrel. Some of those things are quite small, for example worries about the government, bless them, and some are much bigger, like your health or the health of a loved one, losing your job, I don't need to go on probably.

All of these things, big and small, are mixed up in your stress barrel. Everyone has a stress barrel. The people who cope are those whose barrel contains the stress without overflowing. The people who don't cope are the ones whose barrel overflows because there's just too much in it. What you tend to do is concentrate on the big worries but you can't do anything about those usually so the stress barrel remains full.

I want you to list in the barrel everything that is currently making you stressed. And I do mean everything, no matter how insignificant you think it is. This, remember, is the sum of everything in your life that is troubling you. If you could remove all of these worries your life would be completely fine. Right, you've got the idea.

Finished? Now I want you to take a pen and draw a tap on this barrel, somewhere near the bottom, as you would expect on a real barrel. And I want you to look at your collection of stressors in the barrel and ask yourself which ones, if you turned the tap on to let them out, could quite reasonably be dealt with. Which ones are doable? Which ones have you been ignoring because you've been overwhelmed? These are the ones you are going to tackle. Yes, they seem minor to you, but think about the effect on the barrel. The barrel limits the amount of stress you can take without giving in. Create spare capacity in your stress barrel by lowering the level.

And do this regularly, so your stress remains, as far as possible, under control. I think it makes a lot of sense, so do try it.

Learn to alter your stress reaction

Some people react badly to stressors and some don't. I don't know why this is but I suspect it has rather more to do with nature than nurture. I used to be bad at stress, especially driving, which I hate. I resolved the driving stress by changing my car. I bought a big old limousine and in that I felt isolated from other road users. I no longer needed to compete (it couldn't go very fast anyway) and in the days before SUVs the driving position was higher than most other cars.

When I started doing the work I do now two of the doctors I worked with specialised, among other things, in stress management, and we decided to introduce certain techniques into our programmes. Helping people to stop smoking means inevitably that they are under stress (although because we can control the addiction to nicotine this is greatly reduced) so we throw everything into the mix we can find. There are two techniques in particular that you will find helpful, not just for stopping smoking, because they really will help you to be more relaxed and that will always be useful. I do both of these myself, we all do in the Institute, so that tells you they are good.

Breathing

You would be amazed how few people know how to breathe. Prove me wrong. Stand up and take a deep breath. Did your abdomen go in or out as you breathed in? Not sure? Do it again.

If you are anything like 99.9% of our patients, your belly goes in when you breathe in. Well, why not? I'll tell you why not. Blow up a balloon. When you put air into it does it go out or in? Let the air out. Does the balloon go out or in? Fill up your lungs, they get bigger, like balloons, don't they? So why, if your lungs are getting bigger, would your belly get smaller? Aha, you say, because I'm expanding my lungs in my chest, not my belly.

Yes you are. But don't. Under your lungs is a muscular membrane called the diaphragm. This membrane is like a bellows. Above it, your lungs are like long balloons as opposed to round balloons; when they expand they try to expand lengthways as well as outwards. And what are you doing? Yes, you're pulling your abdominal muscles in, which push your diaphragm up - against your lungs, so they can't expand the way they want to.

Pulling your belly in when you breathe in actually limits your lung capacity. Trust me, it's true. Why does this matter? Because when you are stressed your breathing changes; it becomes rapid and shallow. This is because you are producing adrenaline. Stress equals adrenaline. If you can't reduce the stressor what you can do is reduce the adrenaline, by not forcing your body into a stress reaction, by breathing the way you would if you were calm. Calm people breathe deeply, stressed people breathe shallowly. Breathe deeply and you will become calmer.

People always say take a deep breath when you're stressed, don't they? But you can't take a really deep breath unless you use the bellows, your diaphragm, to expand and contract your lungs properly.

This is how you learn to do it. Take a book (preferably not this one, unless you've got a good memory), lie down, and put the book on your belly.

As you breathe in, make the book rise. No, it doesn't seem natural, but in fact it is. How do we know? Look at a small baby breathing in its sleep. Look at a cat or dog sleeping. They all do it. It's something we grow out of because we're so clever.

As you breathe out make the book go down. Once you've got the hang of it do it several times. Learn what it feels like to breathe correctly. Then, you can try it standing up, and you should repeat the exercise for a minute at a time several times a day.

I regularly hold my breath in for sixty seconds, and I've been tested while I do that and my pulse rate drops dramatically. Now, whenever you feel stressed, you can switch on this wonderful technique and switch off your stress reaction. It won't pay the gas bill, but it will make you feel better about not being able to pay it. Use it at night especially if you can't get to sleep.

Shiatsu

We teach this ancient Chinese technique in our clinics because it's easy to learn and very effective, although teaching it in a book isn't as easy as face to face but I think you will get the idea. Shiatsu is a form of acupuncture, sometimes called acupressure, which means using acupuncture points but applying pressure to them instead of needles.

Acupuncture is a brilliant pain and stress relief treatment, so its obvious application when you stop smoking is to help with withdrawal symptoms. Of course it isn't as effective as an acupuncture treatment, but its big advantage is that you can treat yourself, any place, any time.

We teach a number of shiatsu points in our clinics but two will suffice here. When doing shiatsu, do not have your legs crossed.

On the palm of your hand there are various lines. Hold your right hand facing you. The line that starts under your longest finger and goes off in a curve and disappears off the left edge has an acupuncture point on that edge. With the fingers of your left hand tap that point. That's shiatsu. Do it for a few seconds only, and then swap and do the same on the other hand. Always do both sides.

Use this exercise several times a day. Whenever you feel anxious about stopping smoking, spend a minute doing it and think of it as the exercise that takes away that anxiety.

The next shiatsu point is this: on your face, immediately under the centre of your eye on top of the cheekbone. With one finger, tap this point. For added effectiveness, place your other hand flat against your forehead, where there are several acupuncture points which like to feel this slight pressure while you do it. OK, after say fifteen seconds of this, swap hands and do the other side. If you are not sure if you are tapping the correct point, look in a mirror and make sure it's dead centre under the eye.

Do this exercise whenever you feel really wound up, or you can't sleep. It's quite powerful. I usually do the facial point first, and then a deep breathing exercise. They work very well together.

Some people call this Emotional Freedom Technique, or EFT. Personally, I think that's a slightly soppy name that enables people to write books and run classes for a simple, well-understood exercise.

Break the stress/smoking connection

I've said it before and I'll say it again, stress makes people smoke. And I've said before that smoking doesn't make people less stressed, it just fools them into thinking it does. It's a good trick. It's such a good trick that smokers don't believe they will be able to cope with their lives without smoking and then when they do stop and they get stressed they smoke again because they imagine it is somehow going to help.

I am not exaggerating when I say it is the single most important way (after the addiction to nicotine) the tobacco companies keep people buying their drug. It is therefore a very great threat to you stopping smoking and staying stopped. The threat is not, remember, that you need to smoke because you get stressed, but that you imagine you do. That belief is created by the addiction to nicotine, and once you have it you will have it for the rest of your life. If you think I'm making a meal of this unnecessarily I promise you I'm not. You think I've been doing this job all these years and haven't seen it so often I could weep? People who successfully stop smoking and then ring us to say they've started again, but something bad happened. And we say, uhuh, and what's that got to do with starting again, except very often we don't say it we just think it, because what we want to do is knock some sense into them but you can't, especially down the telephone.

We're unusual in the world of smoking cessation, in that we know this happens, we are not surprised when it happens, and in the end we shrug our shoulders and just help them to stop again. But if only we could get people to separate smoking from stress. If only pigs could fly.

Well, having got that off my chest you know what I'm going to say next, don't you? You have to separate smoking from stress. From today on, from this sentence on, you are never again going to imagine that smoking relieves stress, are you? You are never again going to believe a friend who offers you a cigarette when you are stressed and says go on, it's only one, it will help. No it won't.

So first, make a commitment now that you will tell your friends never to offer you a cigarette, not even if they think your life depends on it. If you usually buy your cigarettes from the same tobacconist tell them now that you are stopping smoking and if you come in to buy some they are to refuse to sell them to you. You think I'm joking, don't you? Do I sound like I'm joking?

Cigarettes are not your friend, they are your enemy. If it helps, write this sentence on scraps of paper and make sure you can always see one. And finally, you will find in Project 12 what we call The Four Promises. Learn them, practise them, live your life by them. They might save it one day.

It's time to assess your stress and make a commitment to not smoking because of it. What stressors, using your stress barrel, are you going to eliminate BEFORE you stop smoking?

Project Eight

Control your smoking before you stop

There is a very unfortunate myth put about by people who frankly should be ashamed of themselves. They say you either smoke or you don't, that there's no point cutting down, you've got to stop altogether. Well, let's examine that for sanity. Which would you say is worse, smoking:

5 a day ☐ 20 a day ☐ 50 a day ☐

I'm going to guess that you ticked 50 a day. In which case is it not axiomatic that smoking 20 a day is better, and that smoking 5 a day is better still? Aha, you say, I want to stop altogether. Yes, we'll come to that, but now answer this question:

Would you say that, if you had no intention of stopping, cutting down from 20 a day to 5 is better than continuing to smoke 20?

Yes ☐ No ☐

If the reasons you want to stop smoking are the normal ones - your health, social issues and the financial cost, it must be true that, if you were not able to stop smoking, going down from 20 to five would resolve 75% of each of these problems.

Yes, I know, you want to stop, but patience.

What we have done so far is establish that being a light smoker is better than being a heavy smoker. So, worst case, you don't stop, I want you to make a promise now, to yourself, not to me, that you will, if all else fails, become a light smoker. Look, I know it's not what you want but we have a quaint saying in the Institute that goes like this:

If you can't control how many you smoke, how are you going to control whether you smoke?

So now you are going to look at controlling when you smoke as a prelude, let's say preparation, for stopping. You are going to learn to control when you smoke so that you are better prepared for controlling whether you smoke. Because control is, after all, what it's about, isn't it? No, I know you don't want to do it, but humour me, because funnily enough I do know what I'm doing here. Anyway, what have you got to lose?

The first stage is to learn more about your smoking, and this means keeping a diary. It's easy to do, and actually it's hugely informative, and I think you will enjoy it and even if you don't life isn't supposed to be endless fun, you know, so just do it anyway.

Every time you smoke a cigarette, make an entry in the diary. Printed here is a diary for one day, but some people like to do both a workday and a weekend day which is probably a good idea, and some people like to do it for a whole week because they're masochists but that's their business, but either way just copy it out onto a sheet of paper, which I expect you had thought of already, and you can do as many days as you like.

Why do you want it?	Enjoying it?	Did you need it?

Every time you are about to smoke, but before you light up, take a few seconds to ask yourself why you want it. It should go without saying that you have to be honest, but I'll say it anyway. You have to be honest. Then light it and while you're taking the first few drags write down whether you are enjoying it. Then, when you've smoked at least half of it, I want you to ask yourself the question again and say whether it is STILL enjoyable. There's a good reason for this, naturally, and I'll explain it in a moment. Then, after you put the cigarette out, go to the last column and say whether, on serious reflection, you could have gone without it.

Why do you have to think twice for each cigarette? Because, as you probably know, you get more than one effect from each cigarette. Have you ever had that feeling of relief when you take the first drags, especially if you haven't been able to light one for a while? I'm sure you know what I'm talking about. But have you also noticed that as you smoke more of the cigarette the pleasure, relief, call it what you will, diminishes, that you lose interest in it? You might well carry on smoking it, but now it's not because you want to but because you don't want to waste the money you spent on it.

If this is true for you, then a very important bit of information has been learned already. For you, the pleasure of smoking has nothing to do with the pleasure of smoking, because if it did the pleasure would last for the whole cigarette. The pleasure is, apparently, coming from the inhalation of nicotine. Once you have had a dose of nicotine, the body is a lot less interested in getting more. It doesn't actually need a whole cigarette to get a fix, it just needs a few puffs.

So this part of the exercise has already taught you two

things:

- You don't enjoy smoking for its own sake, which means you don't enjoy smoking.
- You light a cigarette to get a fix of nicotine.

This is terribly important information when it comes to figuring out how you are going to stop smoking, because what have I been saying? That if you understand the reasons you can't stop you will find the answers.

Now I'm going to explain another critical reason for going to the trouble of controlling your smoking. People smoke, say, 20 a day but the reason for some of those cigarettes is different from the reason for others. Your reasons, which you have now learned, might be stress, addictive craving, drinking, socialising, boredom and so on. If you smoke 20 a day and just try to stop smoking, you are actually trying, in your case, to resolve five different issues, all at the same time, and this could be a very good reason why you have failed up until now.

Keeping the diary is going to have done one of two things, or possibly two of two things. It will have shown you what the issues are so you separate them and deal with each one in turn. And it might have enabled you to eliminate some of the issues already, simply by becoming aware of them as you kept the diary.

The end result is that you will not only be smoking far fewer cigarettes than before, but you will also be down to perhaps one major problem, the real reason why you haven't stopped smoking before. You have eliminated the easy problems and now you are left with the hard one. The benefit of this is that before, while you were trying to deal with the hard one, the easier ones kept coming along and getting in the way.

For example, let's say your problem all along has been the addictive craving for nicotine, but while you tried to cope with that you were going to the pub, and seeing people going outside to smoke was just too much for you and you gave in. Well, I know you might not like it but on the basis that every problem has a solution, in this case not going to the pub until you have stopped smoking would eliminate the problem of being triggered by other people smoking and leave you able to concentrate fully on the real issue, which we said in this example was the addiction.

Another example might be helpful? Say you are really stressed at work, and smoking gives you a chance to get out of the office and take a cigarette break. And then after work you reward yourself for getting through the day by going out with your friends for a drink, but they smoke and that undoes your resolve not to. You've got two interconnected issues here, so you need to separate them.

Resolving the problem at work (which I realise might not be possible but I'm a smoking cessation expert, not a careers counsellor) will remove the reason why you smoke during the day, or at least one of the reasons. On the other hand, finding some other way of de-stressing at the end of the work day will resolve the second problem. Or you could ask your friends for their support and still go with them but give them permission to beat you about the head if you ask them for a cigarette.

The purpose of this exercise it to disentangle the web of reasons you can't stop smoking so that, to the best of your ability anyway, you deal with each one separately and eliminate it. This will leave you with the big one, whatever it might be. Only you can work out what it is, but I promise you I know from long experience with thousands of smokers there is usually one main reason why they have failed to stop. If every smoker analysed their smoking in this way, they would, all of them, have a much better chance of stopping.

So you see, I told you I know what I'm talking about. I know you had your doubts, but look, you've got to trust me, OK?

And what are you going to do now? You're going to ignore what I just said? No, I don't think so. What you are really going to do, which I'm sure you meant, is from now on you are going to think before you light every cigarette, and you are going to ask yourself if you really want it, and if you don't you are going to not smoke it. Why? Because, and I have a feeling you've heard this somewhere before, if you can't control when you smoke how are you going to control whether you smoke?

Huh?

**This is one of the most important projects.
Note here the progress you have made with bringing your smoking under control BEFORE stopping.**

Project Nine

The smoke-free day experiment

People who are trying to stop smoking do a strange thing, in my opinion. They try to stop smoking. I mean, why? Especially since they usually fail, and then they are even more afraid to try again. Failure breeds failure. And with smokers it confirms what they always suspected, that they can't stop.

You would be amazed at the number of people who have never tried to stop smoking, and I don't mean people in their twenties, but people in their thirties and older, and they have never actually tried to stop. Why? Well, that question is answered in a number of parts in this Handbook, but for now I want to work with one reason - they don't think they can.

This isn't a good reason to keep smoking. It is self-evidently utterly defeatist. I don't think I could climb Mount Everest so I don't try. Now that is a reasonable way to think. Actually I don't want to either, so that's another reason, but let's stick with I can't so I don't. The point, though, is that climbing Everest has no real benefit. It's not, for example, going to save my life (it could of course do the opposite).

As you now know, thinking you can't stop smoking is part of the fear of stopping, and the belief that you can't is really just an excuse so you don't have to try, but excuse me and I know I promised I wouldn't lecture you but as you know from time to time I have to include a sanity check and we are, let's face it, talking about coming off an addictive drug that is threatening to kill you so let's get serious.

And anyway, a lot of people have tried to stop smoking and have failed. They interpret that, sadly, as meaning they can't stop, but that's not true at all. I failed my first three driving tests but did it mean I couldn't drive? Well, OK, at the time, yes, but since then I passed and have been driving for, well, a long time. Alright, I am the first to admit I'm not a good driver (now did you ever hear a man admit that?) but it doesn't alter the fact that I passed the test.

The relevance if this? Any driving instructor will tell you that failing a test is, for many people, an important part of learning to drive. And failing to stop smoking can and should be an important part of learning to stop. Sadly, what most smokers do, as I said, is use failure to confirm that they are no good at not smoking (yes, when you put it like that it sounds silly) instead of learning from their mistakes. Learner drivers get better the more they try, smokers get worse. Strange.

Anyway, now I want you to try a little experiment, an experiment in succeeding. You can do it whether you have tried to stop before or not. Come on, it's fun.

Alright, fun might be an exaggeration, but would I ask you to do something I wouldn't do myself?

It's called The Smoke-Free Day. It's a catchy name that fairly well encapsulates what it's about, on account of you are going to have a complete day during which you don't smoke. Oh well, I hear you say, is that it? Look, if I could stop, you say ... yes but I didn't say you are going to stop smoking, did I? In fact what you are specifically not going to do is stop smoking. If I wanted you to do that I would say so. What you are going to do is feel what it's like not to smoke for a day. Oho, you say, I know what it's like because I've already tried it. No you haven't. What you've tried is not smoking for a day because you're trying to stop smoking. What this is about is not smoking for a day because you are NOT going to stop smoking. Crazy? No, jam-packed with good sense.

Have you ever been on a long flight, say twelve hours to the US or India, or even longer to Australia or the Far East, and managed without smoking? Have you ever had flu and not smoked for two days? Have you ever gone to sleep and not smoked until the next morning? There are lots of times when you don't smoke for a while, aren't there? And you can do it because you know that afterwards you are going to smoke. Not smoking for a while is a necessity that has nothing to do with stopping, so it's alright. If you knew you couldn't smoke again, ever, when you got off the plane, now that would be completely different, wouldn't it?

It is the fear of success, the fear of stopping smoking, that contributes to the immediate difficulty of not smoking. So the point of this exercise is to feel what it's like not to smoke specifically with the certain knowledge that you are not stopping smoking, that in fact you are going to smoke for sure afterwards, and it has a quite remarkable effect on you. Not smoking for one complete day is something almost any smoker can do, unless you are a heavy smoker, say thirty or more each day, in which case for one day read half a day. No, I said thirty, not twenty. Don't be such a wimp.

Before we look at this in detail, here are some things you can do to help make your Smoke-Free Day a success.

- Decide whether a working day or a weekend day will be easier.
- If you're not working, plan a fun-filled day when you won't be sitting around bored.
- Exercise.
- Drink lots of water.

And now I'm going to make this really easy, so don't say I don't care about you. You can smoke on your Smoke-Free Day. No, this is not a joke. You can, if you want, smoke herbal cigarettes. You see, the point of the Smoke-Free Day is not to not smoke, but to not smoke nicotine. And the point of smoking herbal cigarettes on this day is that they will give you all the psychological support you would get from a real cigarette because smoking is smoking. What you won't be getting is a fix, but because you will be smoking you won't be under pressure to smoke, if you see what I mean. Read the bit about herbal cigarettes again in Project 5.

So now tell me you can't do one day without tobacco. Oh, and by the way I shouldn't have to say this but I will, you can't use an NRP on this day.

During your Smoke-Free Day, write here a brief diary of what it feels like.

The next morning, as early as possible, you are going to smoke a tobacco cigarette, and carry on smoking as normal. At some point during this day, make some comment here about what it feels like to be able to smoke again.

So what have you achieved? I'll tell you. You have practised not smoking without the fear of never smoking again getting in the way. You have experienced one-day's withdrawal symptoms unaffected by any of the issues around actually stopping smoking. How are you going to feel at this point? I haven't a clue. How could I?

But you do. You know if you feel you achieved something. You know now what it is like to experience one issue, a big issue, around stopping smoking separated from the other issues. So now you know the worst it gets.

Now say something about how you feel it went, what you learned, and if it's worth doing again.

Yes, that's right, I said again. You don't think that's it, do you? What you do now depends on how long you think it is going to take you to stop altogether, but I suggest perhaps having a Smoke-Free Day once a week. This will get you comfortable with being in control of tobacco, so it's a major step toward the day you don't go back to smoking.

Oh, and by the way, a nice idea, I think. How much do you spend on smoking? For every Smoke-Free Day you achieve, put those dollars or pounds aside for your favourite charity.

OK, did you really do this project or did you funk it? If you didn't do it, justify yourself. If you did, do you feel it has taken you a step closer to stopping?

Project Ten

Don't stop, just don't smoke

(If you are using a drug product or another programme at the same time, skip this and go straight to Project 11)

If this were any other book about stopping smoking, this is the point where it would say, OK, now you're going to stop smoking, and you would do one of two things:

- You would close the book and put it somewhere you can't find it, so you never have to face up to it.
- You would read this chapter and think, huh, is that the best he can do?

Well, don't close this Handbook because this next bit is not going to frighten you, I promise, and don't say huh either, because I'm going to say something that might surprise you.

In the glossy leaflets printed by government organisations with more money than brains, you know the ones, they've usually got lots of amusing but completely pointless little cartoons, they say set a date for stopping. No, I don't think so. You would rather wrestle with crocodiles than stop smoking and they want you to put a date in your diary? Wrong.

By now, if you're any good at following instructions, you've already done the Smoke-Free Day. On the other hand, maybe you haven't, by which I mean maybe you couldn't. Maybe you tried it and thought, this is silly, why don't I just stop messing about and stop?

Well, make my day.

On the other hand, maybe you did it successfully and you thought, yes, I can do this. Well, great, but don't get carried away. The object of that exercise was for you to challenge yourself without having to stop smoking yet. A bit like getting your friends to lower you into a river full of crocodiles upside down and pulling you out minus just one arm, to see if you like it.

This business of stopping smoking, you know, on the big day, well it's all terribly stressful, and I don't know about you but I'm not a great believer in increasing my stress if I don't have to. So try it a different way.

When you wake up in the morning, you're a non smoker. You haven't lit a cigarette, and by definition that makes you a non-smoker. I know what you're thinking, but stop thinking like that and listen. You're not a smoker until you light a cigarette.

Now, let's say you normally get up at 7.30 and light the first one at 8 o'clock. What is it you normally do just before 8? A shower? OK, have a shower the night before, so now you don't light up after the morning shower because there is no morning shower. Spend that time doing something different. So now you sit down at the kitchen table and you have a cup of coffee. Normally, this would be your second cigarette. Alright, so you light that one. Have you failed?

No, you haven't failed because you weren't trying to do anything. No target, no failure. What you have achieved so far is that you waited half an hour before you smoked the first one of the day.

Day two. Jumble up the morning routine a bit more and who knows, perhaps you don't smoke until you're waiting at the bus stop to go to work. Do this for a week. You know, a lot of people don't smoke first thing in the morning, and you could be one of them. Have to smoke first thing? Well, what about doing it the other way round? The first cigarette of the day is usually the one you need most? Well, smoke it. Aha, you say, if I smoke one I'll carry on smoking.

Really? Why?

So you have the first one, even the first two, but don't smoke the one you normally have on the way to work in the car. In fact put them in the boot so you can't. Are you going to die if you do this? Probably not. Then smoke the rest of the day.

The point of the exercise is not to cut down how many you smoke. Remember, anyone can cut down, and indeed you should have done that by now. The point is not the number you smoke at all, it's something completely different and far more important. I want to remind you of our favourite saying. If you can't control when you smoke, how are you going to control whether you smoke? Your problem before now has always been stopping smoking. You've never had a problem with controlling when you smoke because you've had to do it at work and on public transport and so on, so actually you have more control than you think.

Every smoker has control because they have a brain. You can, in fact, reduce the number you smoke right down to the Addiction Threshold without difficulty, and that, remember, is only four a day. Yes, four.

What you are doing in this important exercise is not smoking when you don't need to, but more importantly deciding when you smoke, changing the times round at will, using tobacco, not being used by it, deciding when to smoke, not being told when to. It might take a week to get to this stage, it might take longer, but however long it takes you should, once you are happy that you've got the hang of it, carry on doing it for another week. I don't want you to get blasé about it. I want you to feel so in control you can do anything, anything at all, because you call the shots.

What I do not want you to do is clockwatch, waiting until you can light the next one. That is not the point at all. The point is to use your new understanding of why you smoke each cigarette, the knowledge you have gained about yourself in previous projects, to smoke, now, only those cigarettes for which you have an addictive craving, which by now you should be able to recognise.

Going through this process, learning to smoke only the ones you need because of a definable craving and not for any other reason, is the biggest thing you will ever do towards becoming a non-smoker. I would go so far as to say that even if on this occasion you don't actually stop smoking you will have changed the smoker you are, for ever.

You will have made a change so profound that at any time in the future you will be able to click your fingers and say pfui, or some such thing, and stop. You will not be afraid to stop smoking because smoking will have lost its control over you.

OK, so much for that, but here you are, feeling good about yourself, thinking yes, this bloke might actually know what he's talking about, sorry I doubted him, but where do you go from here? How do you stop smoking the last few?

Well, as you know, the last four are the ones you need to smoke to prevent withdrawal symptoms. Those last four represent your addiction to nicotine, and they are going to be the hardest to let go of. I could kid you it's going to be easy but I won't, but don't worry, we're going to go through this together. Alright, it's going to hurt you more than it hurts me, but come on, are you really afraid of a little pain?

You are? Well, I don't blame you, but look, you're actually closer to your goal than you might think. You see, although I go on about addiction and withdrawal, it's not that simple.

Withdrawal is a purely physiological reaction, and yes, it lasts for four days, but it's so closely connected with your psychological dependence that normally when people try to stop smoking their psychological dependence actually makes the withdrawal symptoms worse. That might not be strictly true medically, but even so there is a measurable effect. When you are afraid to stop smoking, the withdrawal symptoms might be worse, or at the very least you might feel them more. It makes sense, don't you think?

But you, remember, are no longer afraid. You have conquered tobacco and you have conquered your fear of it. Therefore, you will be pleased to know, even the withdrawal symptoms are going to be lessened; in fact, whilst I can't promise, you might not even have any. How do I know this is true? It's simple to prove. A good hypnotherapist can convince the brain not to feel withdrawal symptoms when you stop smoking. It's mind over matter, and it works. Therefore, if you have come this far with this Handbook and you are in control, that is to some extent like having hypnotherapy. You have a mind and it doesn't matter, or something like that.

So far so good, but it's all about the psychology, so what can you do in practical ways to make the next bit easier?

- Do your stress management exercises from Project 7.
- Make the dietary changes from Tutorial 10, including the business with tomatoes.
- Buy some herbal cigarettes and use them the way I explain in Project 5.
- Ensure your fluid intake is as high as possible.
- Put yourself on a detox regime of vitamin C (we use 3000 mg a day in our clinics, but cut back if you react to this, and high water intake must go with this regime).
- Exercise as much as you feel comfortable with, preferably outdoors, but if you feel tired give in and rest.

Finally, what should you do if it goes wrong? Well, it can't, because you don't have a target. You mean by that if you smoke, don't you? Well, we have a funny attitude to smoking in the Institute. We don't call it failure, ever. You've read about this in Tutorial 12, so I won't bore you here.

Let's start again. What do you do if you smoke? You've got two choices here. You can say oh well that didn't last long, I'll carry on smoking, or you can say oops and carry on not smoking. The point is that smoking, one, or a whole pack, doesn't actually change anything.

Don't, whatever you do, think of this as some kind of test. Read through Tutorial 12 again until you believe it. In short, making a mistake and smoking actually has no bearing on your stop-smoking plan. Which means that everything you do is good. Smoking none is good, and smoking two instead of twenty is also good.

The plan you are following in this Handbook doesn't work or not work. It's an ongoing project. Go back into any part of it as needed and do some more work on yourself. There's an e-mail address in the resource listing at the back if you would like to ask a question, or you can even telephone us to talk it through. We won't mind. We can't promise you'll speak to me personally, but everyone is an ex-smoker who stopped with the help of one of our own programmes, and one thing you can be absolutely certain about is that they will be completely non-judgmental about you. If you feel the NHS smokers' helpline has something to offer, give them a call instead.

Repeat this project every day (but not on the days you don't feel like it) and any day you can't make it work, well, who cares, and every day you can make it work is another day of success. You could say you keep failing because there are days when it doesn't happen, but that's not true. You keep succeeding, because there are days when you don't smoke. Keep doing this and there will come a time, I promise, when every day is a success and you have won. And remember, do if for four consecutive days and on day five you are no longer addicted. Wow.

If you take all of this on board you are, at some time, going to be a non-smoker. Now go straight to Project 12 for detailed instructions for dealing with problems.

Remember, this is not about success or failure. Make an honest assessment here, based on everything you have learned from the Handbook, of your progress so far. If you haven't yet stopped, can you at least see a way forward?

Project Eleven

Just do it anyway

(If you are using a drug product or a therapy you will follow this instead of Project 10)

If you are using, or planning to use, a drug product while you work though the Handbook, you need to look at the instructions you have been given with that product. When using an NRP it is normal to come off tobacco as soon as you start it. The idea of the NRP is to use it to maintain your addiction without the need to smoke. So what should you do if you are on an NRP or a psychotropic drug and you still feel the need to smoke? And does the idea of not smoking, as opposed to stopping smoking, work in this case?

Well, naturally, if you are using such a product and you still want to smoke you need to go back to the pharmacist who supplied it, or even the GP or nurse who prescribed it, because they should have the answers, or you can call the NHS smokers' helpline, because being sponsored by the manufacturers they also should have the answers. Their number is at the end of the Handbook.

The second question is a little trickier. Our philosophy,

and the one I have been encouraging you to adopt in the Handbook, is not to see stopping as a challenge. The problem with challenges is that when people can't cope with them they assume they have failed, whereas if there is no test to start with there is nothing to fail. Unfortunately, the attitude of many NHS staff is still the outdated one of success or failure, so if you are using a drug product (an NRP or a psychotropic drug) my advice is to stay with our philosophy and not go back to your GP or chemist and report failure.

After all, reporting failure serves exactly what purpose? Is it a cry for help or is it a way to blame someone else? So in this situation I am going to suggest you resist the urge to say you have failed, to use the product perhaps in a slightly different way. I'm not allowed to say what you should or shouldn't do with a drug product, so I'm not going to, but I am going to encourage you in this project to look at the problem in a different way.

Actually, I am going to encourage you to continue with your attempt to stop smoking notwithstanding the product. I'm saying that if the product helps you, at all, that's nice, but if it doesn't, or not enough anyway, that you are going to take over from it and you are going to stop anyway, regardless of what the product does or doesn't do.

So this project is about getting what you can out of any drug product or therapy, and applying some other bits as well. Let's look at what you're trying:

Nicotine replacement products

Are you finding it hard to use? This means the patch slips

off or you react badly to it, the gum gives you stomach ache, or the inhalator burns your throat, whatever. In this case, is there any point? No.

So what if you're using an NRP and it is at least not causing any problems? The next questions is, what do you do if it isn't satisfying the craving? Well, this depends on what you mean by craving. The function of an NRP is to feed you with nicotine, and that means, theoretically (definitely theoretically) that you won't have any craving, but do we mean craving for nicotine or craving for a cigarette?

There is an easy way to find out, and this is really important, so do it. Go and buy some herbal cigarettes and, while using an NRP and when you have a strong craving, smoke one. If the craving subsides, it wasn't a craving for the drug, it was a craving to smoke, in other words it was a psychological craving, which of course the NRP is not designed to satisfy.

Now try another experiment. Stop using the NRP for a day and just smoke the herbal cigarettes. If you still have a craving then you need both the drug (from the NRP) and the act of smoking (from the herbal cigarette), so use them together. If you don't have a craving, then you should be able to come off the NRP altogether and just smoke a herbal cigarette from time to time. The need for these will rapidly diminish.

Psychotropic drugs (currently Zyban and Champix/Chantix)

If you are on either of these drugs you have obviously made an informed judgment about taking a drug that changes the way your brain functions in order to stop smoking. Many users are quite anxious about this, and that anxiety can to some extent counter the desired effect of the drug.

If you are having any side effects at all, and by that I mean you are thinking differently, sleeping badly, feeling depressed or having physical symptoms of any kind, you must go straight back to your GP. You want to stop smoking, but there must be a limit to the price you are prepared to pay to do that.

If you can't use these drugs, accept the fact gracefully. If you can, the next stage is coming off them. The most common problem we hear is that the user doesn't smoke as long as they take the drug but starts again when the effect wears off.

If you let this happen you are missing the point. The drug, if it has worked and hasn't caused too many problems, has given you a head start. Don't waste that opportunity. Use everything you have learned in the Handbook to help yourself get the best out of the drug.

Hypnotherapy

Most people do very well, but if you've come out of the session and lit up straight away, does this mean you've failed? Well, yes, probably, but on the other hand are you any worse off than you were before? Yes, I know you are now poorer, but I mean could you go into Project 10 and pretend it didn't happen? No? Why not? Because you're feeling sore about it, probably, but look, are you going to use that as a reason to keep smoking for the next year?

Actually, I will confess what this is about. Alright, you might have just seen a useless therapist, but in our experience that's not often true. What happens more often is that you are managing to reject the therapy. If you decide, right now, to build on the therapy instead, there is a fair chance, a very fair chance, that in Project 10 you will actually do quite well, and that the hypnotherapy you have had will contribute to that more than you might think.

More probably you came out of the session and didn't smoke, perhaps you even felt elated and thought wow, this is great, I feel wonderful and I'm never going to smoke again. Good. Keep going, and especially read Tutorial 12 and do Project 12, because with their help you could stay stopped for ever.

On the other hand, perhaps you did the above and now you're smoking again. At this point you will decide the therapy failed. No, it didn't. It succeeded - you succeeded - but something has happened since (this is a potential problem with hypnotherapy when it's done without follow-up support).

You're thinking can I bear to try stopping again. It's the wrong thing to be thinking. You have already proved you can stop. Now, it's a different issue. It's about staying stopped now, so go straight into Project 12, and if you feel you've slipped too far then go into Project 10 first.

Acupuncture

If you had classical acupuncture (with needles) it probably helped for a while, but there is sometimes only a short-term effect, in which case go back and switch to auricular acupuncture (stud in the earlobe). If you are already on auricular and the studs have fallen off, go back and have them put back on.

If you are using auricular acupuncture and the effect is only limited, consider other tools, especially herbal cigarettes (see above for how to use them), because the acupuncture is probably helping with the withdrawal symptoms but it has no psychological component, which the herbal cigarettes will provide.

Allen Carr's Easyway

If you are reading the Handbook before attending the session, don't be surprised when you go along that what you are told there might contradict some things I have been saying. Easyway is based on some long-standing psychology which still works well for some people, but it is not based on the science we use. So just absorb what you are told there and if you stop immediately that's great in which case focus now on Tutorial 12 and Project 12.

If you have done the Easyway session and not stopped smoking, you could try going back (it's part of their deal) and why not? If you go back and get nothing out of it at all, don't worry; it's a peculiarity of the psychology they use that the more you hear what they say the less effect it has. What you heard is unlikely to have been wasted, because we know that ideas are used in the brain over a very long period. In this case, go back to Project 10, or even consider another therapy, especially if you claim your fee back and so you are now in funds again.

To summarise what I have been saying in this project,

and bore you a little longer, if you are using a drug product or a therapy with the Handbook, and you do well with that product or therapy, use everything you have learned in the Handbook to support it. If you are not doing well, use the Handbook fully, as if you hadn't just had an unsuccessful attempt to stop smoking.

And if you are in a programme from the Institute, you shouldn't have read this project.

If you are using a drug product of any kind, but especially a psychotropic drug, keep a detailed account here of how you feel, both in terms of side effects and whether the drug is helping you.

Project Twelve

Creating a structure for staying stopped

Most of the smokers who come to us have stopped before, so a lot of the work we do, once we've helped them to stop again, is about helping them to stay stopped. In this project you are going to create a structure, one that suits you, that you know you can operate within and fall back on, one that will cover every eventuality, every possible thing that might happen to make you smoke again.

The first thing you are going to do is to write down here the reasons why you have started again in the past, if you have. I hope you don't need all this space.

Not making the same mistakes again is going to depend on you understanding why you made them in the first place, and you should understand that by now from this Handbook. Even as you read them I hope you were thinking to yourself oh yes, now I can see it and I don't think I will fall for that again.

For example, if you started again because you were stressed you should now be saying but I won't smoke next time I'm stressed because I know there would be no point because smoking never really made me less stressed it just tricked me into thinking it did, and in any case there are other and better things I can do when I'm stressed than going back on a drug I spent twenty years trying to get off. Something like that.

For another example, if you do smoke a cigarette and it doesn't taste nice and neither does it make you happier/less stressed/sexier or anything else it promises but doesn't deliver, instead of saying well look I didn't give it a chance, I'd better do it again, you will say to yourself that brilliant Handbook said I should ask myself why, why it doesn't do those things, and the answer is because it can't, it's incapable of delivering anything I want, and I'll put it out and not beat myself up about it. Maybe something like that.

And for yet another example, if you get drunk and smoke and in the morning you realise you've bought some and there they are staring at you, instead of thinking well I've got them so I might as well smoke them you are going to remember the complete futility of that action because you've done it before and instead of making you happy it made you unhappy, and you are going to enjoy throwing them away. Aren't you?

In other words, you are going to look at why you have started again before, in the boxes above, and you are going to not make the same mistake/s again, because now you have more knowledge, a better understanding of what you did and why, and the way to not start smoking again is to not do the same things again.

If you crashed your car because you were talking on the telephone/eating a sandwich/trying to insert a CD/turning round to talk to the children or any other distraction, you will find it a simple matter to assess the cause of the problem, and the way not to repeat the mistake. Now, you are going to do exactly that kind of analysis with smoking. It is something that in all my years doing this work I have never, not once, heard a smoker say they have ever done.

Now, in this box, I want you to write why you want to start smoking again. No, it's not a joke.

So, you didn't write anything in it, huh? Now, write in the next box the reasons why you MIGHT start smoking again.

I would be interested to see if you wrote something because you are genuinely afraid of it, or you wrote nothing because you know there isn't supposed to be anything now and you want to get it right. Well, it's a good job I can't see it, I expect, but what I'm hoping you've written is nothing. You have made mistakes before but there is now no reason for you to repeat those mistakes. Alright, there may be stress, there may be any number of reasons why you would smoke a cigarette because you're not thinking, but there is now no possible reason why, if you make a mistake, you would smoke for the rest of your life, or a year, or even a week, because you have established beyond doubt that:

- You want to be someone who doesn't smoke.
- You know why you got it wrong before.
- You accept that the mistake was a mistake.
- There is therefore no reason to repeat that mistake.

The Four Promises

We ask all our patients to commit to these promises. It would be easy just to say you have to promise never to smoke again, but it would be plain silly, because you could say the words but they wouldn't mean anything. So we break that big one down into four smaller promises, and the good thing about them now is that they are all keepable, and if you keep them you will never become a smoker again. You have to learn them, and you have to become committed to them. Right now.

Promise One
Differentiate between need and want

There you are, watching a friend smoke, or you've been

under stress and you're in the newsagent buying a paper hoping you will give in and buy cigarettes too. You want to smoke. OK, that's almost certainly true. But do you NEED to smoke? Why does that matter? Because you are preparing to go back on an addictive drug that destroys your health and charges you for the privilege. If you don't need it, if you only want it, is that a good reason to die? No, I'm not exaggerating. Is wanting it a good reason to die? Is it possible that the tobacco companies need you right now more than you need them?

Good, you have bought some time by stopping and thinking this through, and the moment passes. Funny, that, isn't it? If you don't smoke, the moment always passes.

Promise Two
If there's no benefit, don't do it

What benefit have you had from being a smoker? What benefit would you get from one cigarette? Aha, you say, but one won't hurt. Let's test that idea. I might step off the kerb with my eyes closed and it might not hurt, because there might be no traffic. But why would I do it? What benefit is there in it? Not why not step off with my eyes closed because it might not hurt, but what would be the point? Saying one cigarette won't hurt is nonsense. And anyway, it might, because it might be the one that turns you back into a smoker and living the last four years of your life on an oxygen cylinder trying to breathe does hurt, so there.

You spent years wanting to stop smoking, and you finally succeeded. Before you throw all that away you have to promise to prove to yourself that there would be a tangible benefit to smoking one cigarette. If you can't do that, and you won't be able to, you have now spent so long thinking about it that the moment has passed. And the moment, remember, always passes.

Promise Three
Listen to your body

OK, you smoked. You forgot the first two promises, or you just had a sod-it moment and lit up. You now have the most amazing opportunity to not make the next mistake, and this is it: how does it taste? Is it nice? Does it relax you? Is it, in short, worth dying for? No, seriously, I mean these words, is it worth dying for?

The chances are, even if you imagine it's some kind of relief, it tastes bad, it makes you cough, go a bit dizzy. Now, you could say wow, the old feeling, great, or you could ask yourself what's happening here.

And what's happening is that you are having a reaction to the 4865 poisons you have just inhaled, and your body is asking you, no, it's begging you, not to do it. Listen to your body, because it knows, better than you do because you're listening to the drug, what's right and wrong. Don't die of stupidity. The first time you smoked, you felt like this but you were too young and foolish to know what your body was trying to tell you. Maybe you stopped some time and started again, and then you didn't do the right thing because you hadn't read this.

Now, you know better. Now, you have a chance not to fall for it again. Don't throw that chance away.

Promise Four
Don't ever light a second cigarette

It is unlikely that the first cigarette you smoke will readdict you. It takes two.

And why, if you have just put a cigarette out and said yuk that was terrible, would you do it again? People do, but they are people who haven't read this. You have read this, and you are not a lemming. Promise, right now, that if you ever smoke, and it isn't nice, that you will put it out and put it behind you. To err is human, but to do it again when you have just received a strong warning not to is madness.

So you see, there is nothing in these four promises that's hard to keep, because they don't preclude the possibility that you will smoke. They almost assume you will, at some time, but they give you a way out of that mistake. They allow you to see that it is a mistake, that it's not what you want. Read them as often as it takes for you to believe them, and promise that from now on you will never, ever, forget them.

Promise Five

Yes, I know it's called the Four Promises, but a chap can change his mind you know, especially when it's as important as this.

Promise yourself that if you ever start smoking again you will deal with it, that you will ask yourself, straight away, if you want to be a smoker or a non-smoker, and if the answer is the latter, which it will be if you are being honest, you will stop there and then. Saying I enjoyed not smoking but now I'm smoking again I might as well carry on is plain bonkers. It is, in fact, doing exactly what the tobacco companies expect and hope you will do, that you will suspend rationality and behave like a junkie.

You will tell yourself that you need to smoke just now because this is a stressful time, regardless of the fact that smoking cannot possibly help you to be less stressed. You won't let this fact get in the way. You will leap over the cliff with the other lemmings because that is what you have been told to do. I think you are worth more than that, don't you?

Promise Six

Will it never end? Look, just one more. I promise.

Promise that once you have stopped smoking you will see yourself not as a smoker who isn't smoking but as, yes, someone who doesn't smoke. Therefore, if you ever make a mistake and smoke, or even have a near miss and are tempted to smoke, that you will think like a non-smoker, that you will not live in fear of starting, because that fear can make you start. That if there is ever a danger that you will smoke, or that you have and might continue, you will ask yourself not do I want to stop again but why would I continue?

Every day people die because they stopped once but started again and they didn't know you are supposed to ask that question. In the box above you wrote the reason why you would want to start smoking again, only there wasn't one, and yet every day thousands, literally thousands, of ex-smokers start again - WHEN THEY DON'T HAVE A REASON TO.

Tobacco is not a friend you miss, is it an enemy. It wants to take over your life, and your job is to prevent it. It is an alien invader, and you have to save the planet, well yourself, by not letting it in. Your ultimate project is the one that is going to save you from this alien invader, that is going to save you perhaps £2000 a year of taxed income, that is going to stop you smelling offensive, that is going to save you from dying of not being able to breathe, that is going to save you from being unhappy about smoking. It is in your hands.

As I write this last paragraph, I am looking out of our office window at a woman who works along the road and comes and stands behind the building for her smoke breaks. I have been out once and asked her if she wants to stop smoking. She says she stopped once but now she doesn't want to. I know she is lying to herself, because you don't stop wanting to be a non-smoker simply because you think you can't, and she has interpreted what she calls failure as meaning she wants to carry on smoking. This woman epitomises everything that is wrong with smoking. I see her smoking several times a day, five days a week, and do you know, I have never once seen her look happy about it.

I said 'I am going to prove you can stop ..', and I also said I was going to tell you things you don't know. OK, how did I do? And more importantly, I said I believe you can stop smoking. Am I right?

Extra Bits

One

Some frequently asked questions

These questions have all, I promise, been asked at some time, in one form or another

If smoking is so dangerous, why do so many people still do it?

Because smoking turns your brain to mush, so you can't think like a non-smoker, and you can't make the same judgments. Smoking is by far the largest example of mass national insanity, even more than voting in General Elections.

If smoking is so dangerous, why does the government allow its sale?

Because governments, bless them, don't, and you might have noticed this yourself, always do the right thing. How can you justify saying that tobacco is addictive and kills 300 users a day in the UK, and allow its sale in sweetshops? You can't. They do. Don't let it worry you, and certainly don't use it as an excuse to carry on smoking. You are right and they are wrong.

What is the point of stopping if I'm under thirty?

If you don't you will be faced with stopping when you are fifty or sixty, when damage will already have been done to your health, and it will be harder to stop. And in any case the question makes no sense. What is the point in NOT stopping?

What is the point of stopping if I'm over sixty?

You have a choice. You can die the easy way or you can die the hard way. OK, you might not have a choice, but if you carry on smoking you certainly won't.

What is the point of stopping if I've already got emphysema?

Emphysema, you will have been informed, is incurable. So why not enjoy smoking while you can? For two reasons. The first is that you don't enjoy smoking, you only imagine you do, and you should certainly by now have understood that.

The second is that emphysema can't be cured, but it can be stabilised. Look at it like this; if you stop smoking it will probably get no worse. If you continue smoking it will. Which do you want?

Isn't smoking really just a habit after all?

Do you really want me to answer that?

So how can I tell if it's habit or addiction that makes me smoke?

Easy. It can't be habit, so it must be addiction, and the dependence the addiction has created.

So why is smoking the only habit I can't control?

Because it is the only habit you have that involves an addictive drug. And anyway, you can control it.

Am I addicted to smoking?

No. You cannot be addicted to an activity. You are addicted to nicotine, which you get from smoking. You are therefore psychologically dependent on smoking to get your drug.

Do I have an addictive personality?

No, for the simple reason that no-one has an addictive personality. You might have a dependent personality, and that might make you more prone to becoming addicted.

Isn't that just semantics?

Yes.

How can some people be social smokers, and could I?

Some people have a high tolerance for withdrawal symptoms, and need nicotine only once every four days. So-called social smokers almost always get nicotine every four days at least, directly or by passive smoking. A small number of those who don't unintentionally remain addicted by eating tomatoes.

By doing this, they can still smoke without displeasure, even after weeks. A small number of people don't do any of this but still 'enjoy' a smoke every few months. No they don't actually. What they do is have a high tolerance for the poisons in tobacco smoke, and the first cigarette, which would normally be unpleasant, is interpreted as a pleasure.

As for you, no you can't. You are addicted, and you can't go backwards from there. Anyway, why would you want to? That you even ask the question confirms that you are afraid of stopping. Once you stop, you will stop being afraid and you won't want to be a social smoker.

How can I stop using cigarettes as rewards?

A cigarette is a reward for not smoking. It is not a reward for finishing the ironing. Check this out by smoking before you finish the ironing.

Why is it I find it easy to cut down from forty to five or six a day but struggle to stop altogether?

Because the first thirty-five you don't smoke are controlled by changing your smoking habits, which is not hard if you have a good reason to do it. You only smoke them because they are there, because you are bored, or tired or stressed, situations you have control over. The last four or five perform a quite different function. They give you the minimum amount of nicotine that will stop you having withdrawal symptoms. Go without one of these and the withdrawal will tell you to smoke. It's like the difference between not overeating and not eating at all.

I've read about something called the Addiction Level. Is this how many cigarettes I smoke or is it the same as the Addiction Threshold?

No, and no. It is an immunological function that is tested by our medical staff for patients in The Phoenix Programme, and doesn't concern you if you're not in it.

Why do you go on about the addiction so much? I've been told it's all in the mind

Well you have been sold a pup. Really, I'm not going to explain it all again. Read the Handbook. But why do people tell you these lies? Usually because they've got a book to sell, or some treatment they've dreamed up, and since they don't understand addiction they sweep it under the carpet. I'm not an uncritical devotee of what often passes for science, but in this case the science just can't be argued with.

How can I control my addiction to nicotine?

There are only three ways that I know of. There are two the Institute provides (Phoenix and acupuncture) and there is the good old-fashioned way, sometimes, for reasons I have never been able to fathom, called cold turkey. Addiction is over in four days. If anyone tells you otherwise they are a nincompoop and you must laugh in their face. If you have still had a craving after more than four days that is either because you were maintaining the addiction by some other means, or you have a craving that has a trigger that is psychological, not physiological.

Does it matter what the trigger is?

Yes.

Why don't I enjoy all the cigarettes I smoke?

This is the acid test for addiction, or one of them. Many of the cigarettes you smoke are for no very good reason, just out of habit because they are there. If you don't need nicotine, you won't much enjoy smoking. If you do need nicotine, because you haven't had any for a while, you will enjoy smoking. The pleasure of smoking is never anything more than the relief of the displeasure of not smoking. Thinking you are enjoying it with friends and a glass of wine is something else, which I have already explained.

Will I enjoy socialising with my friends after I stop smoking?

Look, I don't know your friends, but in short, yes. Don't you enjoy being with your non-smoking friends? Well, all your friends will enjoy being with you when you don't smoke.

Will I be able to play the piano after I stop smoking?

Only if you could before. (Actually, I made this one up. Sorry.)

If I want to stop smoking so much, which I do most of the time, why do I tell myself I don't want to?

This is classic psychological dependence. I've explained it all in detail in this Handbook, but in brief it is because the addiction to nicotine has changed the way you see smoking. On the intellectual level you know smoking is nonsense and you would be better off not doing it, but addiction gets you on the emotional level, and this prevents you approaching the subject rationally. The emotions almost always win over the intellect. Ask anyone who has ever fallen in love. In the words of the goddess of victory, just do it.

What will I do after meals when I no longer smoke?

The washing up.

Why is it I hated smoking at first and now I like it?

Because tobacco smoke is poisonous. You are supposed to hate it. It is still poisoning you, but by becoming addicted you switched off your ability to taste the poisons. You don't like it, you just satisfy the need for it, which is interpreted incorrectly as liking.

How do I know when I've succeeded in stopping? My doctor says it's after a year of not smoking

I'm afraid your doctor is wrong. This one-year business is pseudo-scientific mumbo-jumbo. I can prove it. If I rang you after 364 days and asked you how you were doing and you said fine, not smoking, and then the next day you smoked, are you really going to tell me that means you failed? You succeeded for 364 days, which is all you need to know. Anyone who talks about failure doesn't understand the psychology of smoking and should not be permitted to pretend to offer help to smokers.

And by the way, if you succeed, for a month or even a week, you have succeeded, and if you then smoke, yes you've smoked, but what you have not done is failed, because failed is a meaningless word. If you can stop, and not smoke for one week, you can stop again. So stop worrying about it. And stop expecting your GP to know the answer to everything.

Why do I feel depressed when I stop smoking?

It can happen for a number of reasons. You go through a quite serious physiological change and that can alter your brain chemistry. And suddenly achieving what you have always wanted but were afraid to do is also going to have a effect on you. Perversely, some ex-smokers actually start smoking again rather than go through this life-changing experience. Don't.

I've read there's no point cutting down, you just have to stop

Oh dear oh dear, more nonsense. First, smoking is bad for you, so the less you smoke the less bad it is. Second, if you cut down, say from twenty to ten, you have proved you can control your smoking. Yes, here it comes again - if you can't control when you smoke, how are you going to control whether you smoke?

Got a question? E-mail it to:
handbook@stopsmoking.coop

Two

Where to get help

To get information and advice about any of the products, therapies or programmes mentioned in this Handbook, contact the following:

Nicotine replacement products and psychotropic drugs

You can either ask your GP or practice nurse, or in the UK you can phone the NHS smokers' helpline. This line is sponsored by the pharmaceutical companies so you can be sure they will be able to advise you.

For the same reason though, their sponsors do not permit them to advise on any other stop-smoking method.

The NHS smokers' helpline 0800 1690169

In Scotland the Health Education Board runs Smokeline. They produce a typical waste-of-time booklet, but the last we heard they were not sponsored by drug companies so may give independent advice.

Smokeline 0800 848484

Be aware though that the National Health Service does not like smokers using private services. Your GP is unlikely to talk to you about anything other than drugs, because the NHS pays him or her to promote NHS services, not drug-free solutions.

Allen Carr's Easyway

This business is franchised throughout the UK and internationally.

United Kingdom
www.allencarrseasyway.co.uk

USA and Canada
www.theeasywaytostopsmoking.com

Australia
www.allencarr.co.au

Herbal cigarettes

These are available in most health-food shops, especially Holland & Barrett. The main brand is Honeyrose, who do a good range of flavours as well as a variety of hand-rolling mixtures (which are also useful for rolling joints without tobacco).

United Kingdom
www.honeyrose.co.uk
01473 467949

USA
www.honeyroseusa.com

Acupuncture

In the UK, there are two ways to find a qualified acupuncturist. Look in the Yellow Pages, where you will find a large advertisement for the British Acupuncture Council. All BAcC members are well qualified in acupuncture, but you will need to phone them to ask if they specialise in smoking, because many don't.

If you want acupuncture as part of a programme that includes counselling and support, see the Institute's details below. The NSCI has acupuncturists throughout the UK.

United Kingdom
www.thensci.info
www.acupuncture.org.uk

USA
www.aaaomonline.org
www.medicalacupuncture.org
www.acudetox.com

Canada
www.cmaac.ca
www.afcinstitute.com

Australia
www.acupuncture.org.au
www.acupaa.com.au

Hypnotherapy

In the UK, there are over forty schools of hypnotherapy. They all issue their own certificates, and there is no governing body that controls them. There are at least six societies for hypnotherapists to join, but they do not fulfil the function of a governing body. So how do you find a therapist whose qualifications you can trust? With difficulty.

If you see an advertisement in your local paper suggesting you can stop in a single one-hour session, money-back guarantee, that is just the sort of thing smokers tend to respond to but shouldn't. It is frankly not professional. And if the therapist has a whole string of letters after their name, that doesn't guarantee anything either, unfortunately.

The National Smoking Cessation Institute is the body in the UK that trains and sets standards for hypnotherapists who specialise in smoking cessation. There are NSCI hypnotherapists throughout the UK, and as with acupuncture you will know that there is a comprehensive programme of counselling and support provided with the therapy, as well as having an assurance that the therapist is properly qualified.

United Kingdom
www.thensci.info

USA
www.hypnosis.edu
www.asch.net

Canada
www.archcanada.ca

Australia
www.hypnotherapyaustralia.com.au

The National Smoking Cessation Institute

We are the UK's not-for-profit co-operative doing original research in smoking cessation, as well as working to improve standards, regulate and train therapists, and provide help for those smokers the NHS can't. The Institute is part of the National Smoking Cessation Co-operative.

We are a growing organisation and may have new phone numbers since the publication of this Handbook. It's best to get the latest contact information from our website:

www.thensci.info

Please tell us what you think

I could not have written this Handbook if tens of thousands of smokers had not taught me everything I know. You can help to further build the NSCI Knowledge Base. If you have any comments or suggestions about the Handbook, please don't hesitate to tell us. Do it by e-mail, please, because we can't spend a lot of time talking to readers, as nice as that would be.

Use this e-mail address:

handbook@stopsmoking.coop

Three

Dr Richard Mackarness

Dr Mac, as he is affectionately known by all who came into contact with him, was a consultant psychiatrist at Basingstoke District General Hospital.

As a National Health Service psychiatrist, he got a lot of referrals from physicians who were unable to solve cases and wanted to label their patients' problems as psychological in origin. Dr Mac came to the conclusion that this was incorrect, and his work resulted in an influential book called Not All in the Mind, which explained the triggers for illness that other doctors were missing. The book changed the way many doctors see illness, and became the start of a new branch of medicine called Clinical Ecology, which means looking at the causes of illness instead of just the illness itself, which in turn involves what the lay person calls allergy. It was Dr Mac who saved my life.

His work was not popular with some doctors, because he was saying that rather than prescribing drugs to suppress symptoms, they should spend more time to find what a patient is eating, or breathing, or wearing even, that is triggering their symptoms.

He then brought back from the USA some research that tied in perfectly with his own findings, in particular the amazing fact that allergy and addiction have the same trigger. He realised that they are opposites, which means the same thing - two sides, in other words, of the very same coin. They are both immune-system dysfunction. At the hospital he developed a way to use tobacco, in isopathic titration (the same technique that is used to control allergic reactions), to neutralise tobacco craving, and experimented with this technique with NHS patients, although he could get no funding to further develop the technique into a full-blown smoking cessation programme.

Dr Mac retired to Melbourne, where the State of Victoria Health Commission persuaded him to come out of retirement to do the very work the NHS in Britain would not support, specifically the use of ecological techniques to control addiction, although in Australia in the 1980's this was for heroin and alcohol, not tobacco. He worked there until his death.

The work the Institute has been doing since 1991 is based on the promise I made personally to Dr Mac that his work would continue.

Four

Tobacco neutrogens

Dr Mac's speciality was allergy. He is the doctor who brought from the USA the technique of neutralising allergic reactions with a micro-dose of the allergen, a technique now practised by specialist doctors in the UK.

He theorised that if this can be done for an allergic reaction, it could be done for an addictive one. The reason for this is the close relationship between allergy and addiction. Allergy is when the immune system gives you symptoms of poisoning from a substance that is not a poison. Addiction is the opposite - the immune system telling you, with what we call withdrawal symptoms, that something which is a poison (tobacco in this case) is needed.

Let's start at the beginning. Tobacco smoke is poisonous. You know that because the first time you smoke a cigarette you get the symptoms of poisoning - it tastes bad, it makes you nauseous and dizzy. This is explained fully in Tutorial 5.

When you 'learn' to smoke, what you do is teach your immune system to recognise the poisons you are inhaling and to stop it telling you they are dangerous. You are now addicted.

If you could tell your immune system that you don't need the poisons (such as nicotine), your body would stop asking for them. In other words it would stop sending messages of craving to your brain - the messages that, if you ignore them, create withdrawal symptoms.

Dr Mac hypothesised that if it is possible to block the body's reaction to an allergen, it might also be possible to block the body's reaction to the opposite - withdrawal. He titrated tobacco smoke in water and measured it against the patient's immune reaction to tobacco. He tried it on three hundred patients at the hospital, and in every case, without exception, the patients said it stopped their craving.

This is the foolproof treatment the NHS refused to fund, and that we in the National Smoking Cessation Institute further developed into Addiction Neutralisation Therapy, part of The Phoenix Programme. We only use it for tobacco but the same technique will bring an addict off any substance immediately, and without withdrawal symptoms. The reason the technique is not used by doctors in the NHS is simply because it cannot be patented. Pharmaceutical companies don't produce anything that can't be patented.

This is the QR code for the Institute's website.
If you have a smartphone, you should be able to use it to access websites via QR codes.

iPhone / iPad/iPod Touch
Download Mobiletag Barcodes Reader from the iTunes App Store.

Android
Download the Barcode Scanner App from the Android Market.

Blackberry
Download Mobiletag Barcodes Reader from the Blackberry Appworld.

Windows Mobile
Download QuickMark from
www.quickmark.cn/En/basic/download.asp

Nokia
Some Nokia smartphones can run Mobiletag Barcodes Reader available from the Ovi Store.